Practice Behaviors Work

M000250881

Direct Social Work Practice

NINTH EDITION

Dean H. Hepworth

Emeritus, University of Utah and Arizona State University

Ronald Rooney

University of Minnesota

Glenda Dewberry Rooney

Augsburg College

Kimberly Strom-Gottfried

University of North Carolina at Chapel Hill

Prepared by

Ronald Rooney

University of Minnesota

Glenda Dewberry Rooney

Augsburg College

Kimberly Strom-Gottfried

University of North Carolina at Chapel Hill

BROOKS/COLE
CENGAGE Learning

Australia • Brazil • Japan • Korea • Mexico • Singapore • Spain • United Kingdom • United States

For product information and technology assistance, contact us at
**Cengage Learning Customer & Sales Support,
1-800-354-9706**

For permission to use material from this text or product, submit all requests online at **www.cengage.com/permissions**
Further permissions questions can be emailed to
permissionrequest@cengage.com

ISBN-13: 978-1-133-37169-4
ISBN-10: 1-133-37169-8

Brooks/Cole Cengage Learning
20 Davis Drive
Belmont, CA 94002-3098
USA

Cengage Learning is a leading provider of customized learning solutions with office locations around the globe, including Singapore, the United Kingdom, Australia, Mexico, Brazil, and Japan. Locate your local office at: **www.cengage.com/global**

Cengage Learning products are represented in Canada by Nelson Education, Ltd.

To learn more about Brooks/Cole, visit
www.cengage.com/brookscole

Purchase any of our products at your local college store or at our preferred online store
www.cengagebrain.com

Printed in the United States of America
2 3 4 5 6   19 18 17 16 15

Dear Social Work Student,

Welcome to the *Practice Behaviors Workbook* for Hepworth/Rooney/Rooney/Strom-Gottfried's *Direct Social Work Practice*, 9e. Throughout your course you will acquire a great deal of new knowledge, including an introduction to new theories, informative research, and practical skills like critical thinking skills and frameworks for appreciating and overcoming challenges. All of the knowledge you gain will offer you a deeper, richer understanding of social work. Used in conjunction with your text and other resources, the *Practice Behaviors Workbook* presents you with Practice Exercises that will teach you how to transform your new knowledge into social work Practice Behaviors.

About Competence and Practice Behavior
In social work, the words Competence and Practice Behavior have a unique meaning beyond the typical dictionary definitions. "Competence" in the usual sense means that a person possesses suitable skills and abilities to do a specific task. A competent baseball player must move quickly, catch, throw, and play as part of a team. They also have to think quickly, understand the rules of the game, and be knowledgeable of their environment. In the same way, a competent social worker should be able to do a number of job-related duties, think critically, and understand the context of their work. The Council on Social Work Education (CSWE) has defined specific Core Competency areas for all social work students, and their corresponding Practice Behaviors as follows:

Competencies and Practice Behaviors
2.1.1 Identify as a Professional Social Worker and Conduct Oneself Accordingly
a. Advocate for client access to the services of social work
b. Practice personal reflection and self-correction to assure continual professional development
c. Attend to professional roles and boundaries
d. Demonstrate professional demeanor in behavior, appearance, and communication
e. Engage in career-long learning
f. Use supervision and consultation
2.1.2 Apply Social Work Ethical Principles to Guide Professional Practice
a. Recognize and manage personal values in a way that allows professional values to guide practice
b. Make ethical decisions by applying standards of the National Association of Social Workers Code of Ethics and, as applicable, of the International Federation of Social Workers/ International Association of Schools of Social Work Ethics in Social Work, Statement of Principles

iii

c.	Tolerate ambiguity in resolving ethical conflicts
d.	Apply strategies of ethical reasoning to arrive at principled decisions
2.1.3	**Apply Critical Thinking to Inform and Communicate Professional Judgments**
a.	Distinguish, appraise, and integrate multiple sources of knowledge, including research-based knowledge and practice wisdom
b.	Analyze models of assessment, prevention, intervention, and evaluation
c.	Demonstrate effective oral and written communication in working with individuals, families, groups, organizations, communities, and colleagues
2.1.4	**Engage Diversity and Difference in Practice**
a.	Recognize the extent to which a culture's structures and values may oppress, marginalize, alienate, or create or enhance privilege and power
b.	Gain sufficient self-awareness to eliminate the influence of personal biases and values in working with diverse groups
c.	Recognize and communicate their understanding of the importance of difference in shaping life experiences
d.	View themselves as learners and engage those with whom they work as informants
2.1.5	**Advance Human Rights and Social and Economic Justice**
a.	Understand the forms and mechanisms of oppression and discrimination
b.	Advocate for human rights and social and economic justice
c.	Engage in practices that advance social and economic justice
2.1.6	**Engage in Research-Informed Practice and Practice-Informed Research**
a.	Use practice experience to inform scientific inquiry
b.	Use research evidence to inform practice
2.1.7	**Apply Knowledge of Human Behavior and the Social Environment**
a.	Utilize conceptual frameworks to guide the processes of assessment, intervention, and evaluation
b.	Critique and apply knowledge to understand person and environment
2.1.8	**Engage in Policy Practice to Advance Social and Economic Well-Being and to Deliver Effective Social Work Services**
a.	Analyze, formulate, and advocate for policies that advance social well-being
b.	Collaborate with colleagues and clients for effective policy action
2.1.9	**Respond to Contexts that Shape Practice**
a.	Continuously discover, appraise, and attend to changing locales, populations, scientific and technological developments, and emerging societal trends to provide relevant services
b.	Provide leadership in promoting sustainable changes in service delivery and practice to improve the quality of social services
2.1.10	**Engage, Assess, Intervene, and Evaluate with Individuals, Families, Groups, Organizations and Communities**
a.	Substantively and affectively prepare for action with individuals, families, groups, organizations, and communities
b.	Use empathy and other interpersonal skills
c.	Develop a mutually agreed-on focus of work and desired outcomes
d.	Collect, organize, and interpret client data
e.	Assess client strengths and limitations
f.	Develop mutually agreed-on intervention goals and objectives
g.	Select appropriate intervention strategies
h.	Initiate actions to achieve organizational goals

i.	Implement prevention interventions that enhance client capacities
j.	Help clients resolve problems
k.	Negotiate, mediate, and advocate for clients
l.	Facilitate transitions and endings
m.	Critically analyze, monitor, and evaluate interventions

Each of the Exercises in the *Practice Behaviors Workbook* will focus on learning and applying social work Practice Behaviors. While every Exercise will not ask you to apply Competencies or Practice Behaviors from every Core Competency area, by the time you finish your course you will have practiced many and gained a better working knowledge of how social work is done. The goal, shared by your professors, your program, the authors of this text, and by Brooks/Cole, Cengage Learning Social Work team, is that by the end of your curriculum you will have honed your Practice Behaviors in all of the Core Competency areas into a skill set that empowers you to work effectively as a professional social worker.

Assessing Competence: Partnering with Your Instructor and Peer Evaluator
As described above, the Council on Social Work Education clearly defines the Competencies and Practice Behaviors that a social work student should be trained to employ. Therefore, the grading rubric that comes at the end of every chapter of the *Practice Behaviors Workbook* is adapted from Competencies and Practice Behaviors defined by CSWE (see the table above). To assess your competence during your course, we recommend you partner with a peer(s) who can act as your course "evaluator(s)" to genuinely assess both your written assignments and your role-plays; be sure to ask your professor to comment on and approve the assessments once they are completed by you and your Evaluator. It is our hope that partnering with your classmates in this way will familiarize you with the unique learning opportunity you will have in your Field Experience – the signature pedagogy of social work education. There you will apply all of your knowledge and skills under the supervision of your Field Instructor and Field Liaison before completing your required curriculum.

As always, we thank you for your commitment to education and to the profession. Enjoy your course, and *feel empowered to help others*!

Contents

Chapter 1	
The Challenges of Social Work	

Exercise 1.1	
What is a Client?	

Goal: To distinguish pressures facing potential clients and how they are viewed by social workers.

Focus Competencies or Practice Behaviors:
- EP 2.1.9 Social workers respond to contexts that shape practice.
- EP 2.1.10a substantively and affectively prepare for action with individuals, families, groups, organizations and communities

In chapter 1, distinctions are made between applicants, legally mandated and non voluntary clients. Review the following scenarios and assign their beginning status. Note that voluntarism often varies over time with clients become more or less voluntary. Decide which categories best apply to each situation.

1. Charlotte, 33, is hospitalized for cystic fibrosis, a debilitating illness. As part of her medical treatment, she is entitled to social work services. Applicant __ legally mandated __ non voluntary ___

2. Linda is an 18-year-old adolescent attending high school. She is referred to social services because of frequent absences and her alleged use of marijuana. Linda acknowledges frequent conflicts at home with her mother and is eager to complete her high school degree, move out and get a job. Applicant __ legally mandated __ non voluntary ___

3. Robert, 45, has applied to your community assistance agency where a student intern is placed for a cash grant to assist in paying a large water bill. Services are available to prevent foreclosure; clients must have a credible plan for how grants in addition to their own plans for raising funds will help them avoid foreclosure. Applicant __ legally mandated __ non voluntary ___

4. Dolores, 32, is a heavy user of prescription tranquilizing medication. Her doctor wants her use to diminish. She is often depressed and unhappy about her living situation, living in a new part of the country where she is not accustomed to the weather. She has few friends and stays at home caring for her children. She sometimes thinks about continuing her education. She is referred to social services by her doctor. Applicant __ legally mandated __ non voluntary ___

5. Tom, is a 23-year-old, single male, who is unemployed and has no familial support. He is currently a patient in a chemical dependency unit, or detox unit. He admitted himself seeking detoxification. He is addicted to methamphetamines, alcohol, and opiates. He is also being treated for a schizo-affective disorder and a bipolar-affective disorder, for which he is being medicated. He had been abstinent for two years and has returned to usage; he says that he wants to abstain from usage. The immediate cause of his coming in was having no place to stay, having been kicked out of the place he was living. He did not want to live on the streets in the winter. You are a case worker on the chemical dependency unit and need to assist with discharge planning. Applicant __ legally mandated __ non voluntary ___

6. Angie, 28, comes to a private multi-purpose counseling agency reporting that she is lonely, pregnant, and has relationship issues. She has been having panic attacks on and off for the past two years, since she divorced her husband. She continues to have the panic attacks somewhat related to a new relationship. She has a four year old and is concerned about her ability to parent when she is having panic attacks. She described her panic attacks as being related to severe anxiety regarding the future of her relationship and career. She described these attacks as being physically scary periods of time that last from a few minutes to a few hours when she is unable to function and to calm herself down. She also has shortness of breath and feels out of control while they are happening. Applicant __ legally mandated __ non voluntary __

Exercise 1.2
Engaging Diversity

Goal: To explore ways social workers can interact with clients who differ from them one at least one key characteristic.

Focus Competencies or Practice Behaviors:
- EP 2.1.4 Engage diversity and difference in practice.
- EP 2.1.2 Apply social work ethical principles to guide professional practice.

View the video "Working with Yanping" in which the social worker, Kim Strom Gottfried, conducts an initial interview with Yanping, an exchange student from the Republic of China.

1. What role does the value of client self-determination play in the interview with Yanping?
2. How does Kim assess the context of Yanping's concerns?
3. How does Kim explore expectations and roles?

Focus Competencies or Practice Behaviors:
- EP 2.1.7 Apply knowledge of human behavior and social environment.
- EP 2.1.2 Apply social work ethical principles to guide professional practice.

We present in chapter 1 organizing concepts from systems theory that are useful in organizing social work actions. Target, action, client, and agency systems can often be usefully identified. Analyze the following case example and identify those systems. It can also be useful to clarify who perceives a problem. That is, sometimes family members and professionals may perceive one problem and potential clients may perceive another or have no concern.

Bertha, 86, lives alone in a senior living facility. She was referred to Friends of the Elderly, a supportive service for elders. This occurred because a staff member of the development made an outreach home visit to Bertha and wondered whether she might have unresolved grief over the death of her brother and mother over the past 10 years. When Bertha met with Regina, a social work student intern, she identified her concerns as a depressed mood and loneliness. Bertha had been a caregiver for her mother for 10 years and describes her as the best friend she had in her life. Bertha reports that she would like to get out more often, have stimulating conversations, go to the grocery store and pick her own produce. She agreed to work with her social work intern to address the concerns she had identified. Bertha decided to attend exercise classes as a way of getting out and meeting more people. She also signed up for and participated in computer classes with a tutor as a way of having more contact with people. As a result of their sessions together with the intern, Bertha reported that her mood was improved. She was now initiating conversations with other residents and had scheduled some luncheon engagements with other residents. She now attended exercise class regularly

1. What problems or concerns did Bertha perceive?

2. What problems or concerns were perceived by the referring worker?

3. Who is in the client system?

4. What is the target system?

5. What is the action system?

6. What is the agency system?

7. What potential conflicts might emerge when the referring worker or agency perceive concerns differently than the potential client?

8. What could happen if the potential clients own identified concerns are not addressed?

Focus Competencies or Practice Behaviors:
- EP 2.1.5. Social workers act to advance human rights and social and economic justice

On page 6 of chapter 1, we refer to discussion which has occurred within and outside social work about the meaning of a commitment to human rights and social and economic justice.

1. Describe what is meant by a professional commitment to social justice.

2. What is meant by professional commitment to economic justice?

3. What has been the perception or understanding of persons around you about what it means to be a social worker? It is not uncommon for those surrounding beginning social workers to perceive that you will work in "welfare" and perhaps question your motivation for doing so.

4. How have you explained your commitment to wish to become a social worker?

5. The social work profession has taken a position in support of economic security related to such issues as livable wage, pay equity, job discrimination, social security, and access to health care. Do you perceive this position as a political commitment?

Exercise 1.5 Social work involvement in research informed practice and practice informed research

Focus Competencies or Practice Behaviors:
- EP 2.1.6. Social workers engage in research informed practice and practice informed research

As you learned from the text, social worker use research to inform practice and practice to inform research.

1. Describe the process model of evidence based practice. What would a social worker do who was employing such a model?

2. What are benefits and possible drawbacks of employing an evidence based practice approach with a particular client situation?

3. What are the benefits of research as one source to inform practice?

4. What are the benefits of practice as one source to inform the direction of research?

Chapter 1
Competencies/Practice Behaviors Exercises Assessment:

Name: _____ **Date:** _____

Supervisor's Name: _____

Focus Competencies:
- EP 2.1.2 Apply social work ethical principles to guide professional practice
- EP 2.1.4 Engage diversity and difference in practice.
- EP 2.1.5. Social workers act to advance human rights and social and economic justice
- EP 2.1.6. Social workers engage in research informed practice and practice informed research
- EP 2.1.7 Apply knowledge of human behavior and social environment.
- EP 2.1.9 Social workers respond to contexts that shape practice.
- EP 2.1.10a substantively and affectively prepare for action with individuals, families, groups, organizations and communities

Instructions: Evaluate your work or your partner's work in the Focus Practice Behaviors by completing the Practice Behaviors Assessment form below. What other Practice Behaviors did you use to complete these Exercises? Be sure to record them in your assessments. Please note that as you are beginning your work in this course, high level attainment of competencies at this point in your program is not anticipated. Over the course of this course and this program, your proficiency should increase to the point that you and other competent assessors will agree that you have attained the competency at a satisfactory level.

1.	I have attained this competency/practice behavior (in the range of 80 to 100%)
2.	I have largely attained this competency/practice behavior (in the range of 60 to 80%)
3.	I have partially attained this competency/practice behavior (in the range of 40 to 60%)
4.	I have made a little progress in attaining this competency/practice behavior (in the range of 20 to 40%
5.	I have made almost no progress in attaining this competency/practice behavior (in the range of 0 to 20%)

EPAS 2008 Core Competencies & Core Practice Behaviors	Student Self Assessment						Evaluator Feedback
Student and Evaluator Assessment Scale and Comments	0	1	2	3	4	5	Agree/Disagree/Comments
EP 2.1.1 Identify as a Professional Social Worker and Conduct Oneself Accordingly							
a. Advocate for client access to the services of social work							
b. Practice personal reflection and self-correction to assure continual professional development							

c. Attend to professional roles and boundaries						
d. Demonstrate professional demeanor in behavior, appearance, and communication						
e. Engage in career-long learning						
f. Use supervision and consultation						
EP 2.1.2 Apply Social Work Ethical Principles to Guide Professional Practice						
a. Recognize and manage personal values in a way that allows professional values to guide practice						
b. Make ethical decisions by applying NASW Code of Ethics and, as applicable, of the IFSW/IASSW Ethics in Social Work, Statement of Principles						
c. Tolerate ambiguity in resolving ethical conflicts						
d. Apply strategies of ethical reasoning to arrive at principled decisions						
EP 2.1.3 Apply Critical Thinking to Inform and Communicate Professional Judgments						
a. Distinguish, appraise, and integrate multiple sources of knowledge, including research-based knowledge and practice wisdom						
b. Analyze models of assessment, prevention, intervention, and evaluation						
c. Demonstrate effective oral and written communication in working with individuals, families, groups, organizations, communities, and colleagues						
EP 2.1.4 Engage Diversity and Difference in Practice						
a. Recognize the extent to which a culture's structures and values may oppress, marginalize, alienate, or create or enhance privilege and power						
b. Gain sufficient self-awareness to eliminate the influence of personal biases and values in working with diverse groups						

c. Recognize and communicate their understanding of the importance of difference in shaping life experiences							
d. View themselves as learners and engage those with whom they work as informants							
EP 2.1.5 Advance Human Rights and Social and Economic Justice							
a. Understand forms and mechanisms of oppression and discrimination							
b. Advocate for human rights and social and economic justice							
c. Engage in practices that advance social and economic justice							
EP 2.1.6 Engage in Research-Informed Practice and Practice-Informed Research							
a. Use practice experience to inform scientific inquiry							
b. Use research evidence to inform practice							
EP 2.1.7 Apply Knowledge of Human Behavior and the Social Environment							
a. Utilize conceptual frameworks to guide the processes of assessment, intervention, and evaluation							
b. Critique and apply knowledge to understand person and environment							
EP 2.1.8 Engage in Policy Practice to Advance Social and Economic Well-Being and to Deliver Effective Social Work Services							
a. Analyze, formulate, and advocate for policies that advance social well-being							
b. Collaborate with colleagues and clients for effective policy action							
EP 2.1.9 Respond to Contexts that Shape Practice							
a. Continuously discover, appraise, and attend to changing locales, populations, scientific and technological developments, and emerging societal trends to provide relevant services							
b. Provide leadership in promoting sustainable changes in service delivery and practice to improve the quality of social services							

EP 2.1.10 Engage, Assess, Intervene, and Evaluate with Individuals, Families, Groups, Organizations and Communities							
a. Substantively and affectively prepare for action with individuals, families, groups, organizations, and communities							
b. Use empathy and other interpersonal skills							
c. Develop a mutually agreed-on focus of work and desired outcomes							
d. Collect, organize, and interpret client data							
e. Assess client strengths and limitations							
f. Develop mutually agreed-on intervention goals and objectives							
g. Select appropriate intervention strategies							
h. Initiate actions to achieve organizational goals							
i. Implement prevention interventions that enhance client capacities							
j. Help clients resolve problems							
k. Negotiate, mediate, and advocate for clients							
l. Facilitate transitions and endings							
m. Critically analyze, monitor, and evaluate interventions							

Chapter 2
Direct Practice: Domain, Practice and Roles

Exercise 2.1
Distinguishing Direct and Clinical Practice

Goal: To distinguish definitions and domains of direct and clinical practice.

Focus Competencies or Practice Behaviors:
- EP 2.1.9 Social workers respond to contexts that shape practice.
- EP 2.1.10a substantively and affectively prepare for action with individuals, families, groups, organizations and communities

In chapter 2, the meaning of direct and clinical practice are discussed on pages.

1. Define clinical practice. How is clinical practice described in your field agency?

2. Define direct practice:

3. What role does assessment of mental health needs play in the functions of your field practice agency?

4. Describe the relationship of clinical and direct practice.

5. Should all practice be considered clinical?

Exercise 2.2
What Roles Do We Play?

Goal: To explore various roles performed by social workers.

Focus Competencies or Practice Behaviors:
- EP 2.1.10.k social workers negotiate, mediate and advocate for clients4 Engage diversity and difference in practice.
- EP 2.1.10. Social workers engage, assess, intervene and evaluate with individuals families and groups.

Content on social work roles is reviewed in your text. Review the following vignettes and select the roles which might be employed in each situation.

1. An elderly person is hospitalized for a medical concern. When her time to leave the hospital is approaching, decisions have to be made about where she will go next. Will she go home alone? Will she be assisted by family? Will she go to a nursing home? Which social work roles are most likely to be called upon?

2. You work for a private agency that provides mentoring services for children in kinship care. Kinship care is provided for children who can not currently return to live with their parents. The care is provided by a relative. These services require considerable financial support to operate. Your agency wants you to write a grant to United Way and other possible funders. You are aware that these funders will be interested in knowing what the data suggests regarding effectiveness of any programs that they might choose to fund. Which social work roles are most likely to be called upon?

3. Children who are truant elicit a response from both the school system and the child welfare system. Consider the roles in the two systems that may be called on to address the truancy problem.

4. Your field agency provides linkages to housing services for homeless persons with special emphasis on those with multiple barriers to housing such as diagnosed mental illness. Which social work roles are most likely to be called upon?

5. Your field agency provides counseling and advocacy services to children, youth and families from a faith based orientation. Which social work roles are most likely to be called upon?

6. Your field agency is a multiple purpose ethnic organization offering services to family members across the life span. Which social work roles are most likely to be called upon?

7. Your field agency provides home health care services designed to assist elder and disabled clients in living safely in their homes. Which social work roles are most likely to be called upon?

Goal: To explore various roles performed by social workers in specific case situation

Focus Competencies or Practice Behaviors:
- EP 2.1.10.k social workers negotiate, mediate and advocate for clients.
- EP 2.1.10. Social workers engage, assess, intervene and evaluate with individuals families and groups.

Ali meets with the Corning family in the video "Work with the Corning Family".

1. How does Ali describe functions performed by her agency? What social work roles are performed?

2. What roles does Ali perform with the Corning family?

3. What benefits can there be for a family if an agency performs multiple social work roles? Can you describe an instance of a family benefiting from multiple functions or roles performed by an agency?

Exercise 2.4
Direct Service Provision

Goal: To explore direct service provision roles

Focus Competencies or Practice Behaviors:
- EP 2.1.10a Substantively and affectively prepare for action with individuals, families, groups, and communities.

On page 30 of chapter 2, direct practice roles are delineated. .

1. Delineate the modes of service delivery performed by direct service providers.

2. Performing the role of educator or disseminator of information can be a significant direct service role. How is this role performed in your field agency?

3. Direct services are often delivered to individuals, couples, families and groups in social service agencies. What varied services in these modalities have you observed? Do the same social workers operate with different modalities i.e. working with individuals, couples, families or groups?

Focus Competencies or Practice Behaviors:
- EP 2.1.10.k social workers negotiate, mediate and advocate for clients.

On page 30 of the text, systems linkage roles are described.

1. Delineate the systems linkage roles that social workers perform.

2. Skill in identifying appropriate resources and linking clients to them is often identified as a source of skill and knowledge that is ascribed to the social work profession by other helping professionals. How have you seen staff in your field practicum perform these roles?

3. How does performance of this role link with the social work value of social and economic justice?

<table>
<tr><td colspan="2" align="center">**Chapter 2**
Competencies/Practice Behaviors Exercises Assessment:</td></tr>
</table>

Name: _____ Date: _____

Supervisor's Name: _____

Focus Competencies:
- EP 2.1.9 Social workers respond to contexts that shape practice.
- EP 2.1.10a substantively and affectively prepare for action with individuals, families, groups, organizations and communities
- EP 2.1.10.k social workers negotiate, mediate and advocate for clients.

Instructions: Evaluate your work or your partner's work in the Focus Practice Behaviors by completing the Practice Behaviors Assessment form below. What other Practice Behaviors did you use to complete these Exercises? Be sure to record them in your assessments. Please note that as you are beginning your work in this course, high level attainment of competencies at this point in your program is not anticipated. Over the course of this course and this program, your proficiency should increase to the point that you and other competent assessors will agree that you have attained the competency at a satisfactory level.

1.	I have attained this competency/practice behavior (in the range of 80 to 100%)
2.	I have largely attained this competency/practice behavior (in the range of 60 to 80%)
3.	I have partially attained this competency/practice behavior (in the range of 40 to 60%)
4.	I have made a little progress in attaining this competency/practice behavior (in the range of 20 to 40%
5.	I have made almost no progress in attaining this competency/practice behavior (in the range of 0 to 20%)

EPAS 2008 Core Competencies & Core Practice Behaviors	Student Self Assessment						Evaluator Feedback
Student and Evaluator Assessment Scale and Comments	0	1	2	3	4	5	Agree/Disagree/Comments
EP 2.1.1 Identify as a Professional Social Worker and Conduct Oneself Accordingly							
a. Advocate for client access to the services of social work							
b. Practice personal reflection and self-correction to assure continual professional development							
c. Attend to professional roles and boundaries							
d. Demonstrate professional demeanor in behavior, appearance, and communication							

e. Engage in career-long learning							
f. Use supervision and consultation							
EP 2.1.2 Apply Social Work Ethical Principles to Guide Professional Practice							
a. Recognize and manage personal values in a way that allows professional values to guide practice							
b. Make ethical decisions by applying NASW Code of Ethics and, as applicable, of the IFSW/IASSW Ethics in Social Work, Statement of Principles							
c. Tolerate ambiguity in resolving ethical conflicts							
d. Apply strategies of ethical reasoning to arrive at principled decisions							
EP 2.1.3 Apply Critical Thinking to Inform and Communicate Professional Judgments							
a. Distinguish, appraise, and integrate multiple sources of knowledge, including research-based knowledge and practice wisdom							
b. Analyze models of assessment, prevention, intervention, and evaluation							
c. Demonstrate effective oral and written communication in working with individuals, families, groups, organizations, communities, and colleagues							
EP 2.1.4 Engage Diversity and Difference in Practice							
a. Recognize the extent to which a culture's structures and values may oppress, marginalize, alienate, or create or enhance privilege and power							
b. Gain sufficient self-awareness to eliminate the influence of personal biases and values in working with diverse groups							

- 14 -

c. Recognize and communicate their understanding of the importance of difference in shaping life experiences							
d. View themselves as learners and engage those with whom they work as informants							
EP 2.1.5 Advance Human Rights and Social and Economic Justice							
a. Understand forms and mechanisms of oppression and discrimination							
b. Advocate for human rights and social and economic justice							
c. Engage in practices that advance social and economic justice							
EP 2.1.6 Engage in Research-Informed Practice and Practice-Informed Research							
a. Use practice experience to inform scientific inquiry							
b. Use research evidence to inform practice							
EP 2.1.7 Apply Knowledge of Human Behavior and the Social Environment							
a. Utilize conceptual frameworks to guide the processes of assessment, intervention, and evaluation							
b. Critique and apply knowledge to understand person and environment							
EP 2.1.8 Engage in Policy Practice to Advance Social and Economic Well-Being and to Deliver Effective Social Work Services							
a. Analyze, formulate, and advocate for policies that advance social well-being							
b. Collaborate with colleagues and clients for effective policy action							
EP 2.1.9 Respond to Contexts that Shape Practice							
a. Continuously discover, appraise, and attend to changing locales, populations, scientific and technological developments, and emerging societal trends to provide relevant services							

b. Provide leadership in promoting sustainable changes in service delivery and practice to improve the quality of social services							
EP 2.1.10 Engage, Assess, Intervene, and Evaluate with Individuals, Families, Groups, Organizations and Communities							
a. Substantively and affectively prepare for action with individuals, families, groups, organizations, and communities							
b. Use empathy and other interpersonal skills							
c. Develop a mutually agreed-on focus of work and desired outcomes							
d. Collect, organize, and interpret client data							
e. Assess client strengths and limitations							
f. Develop mutually agreed-on intervention goals and objectives							
g. Select appropriate intervention strategies							
h. Initiate actions to achieve organizational goals							
i. Implement prevention interventions that enhance client capacities							
j. Help clients resolve problems							
k. Negotiate, mediate, and advocate for clients							
l. Facilitate transitions and endings							
m. Critically analyze, monitor, and evaluate interventions							

Chapter 3
Overview of the Helping Process

Exercise 3.1
Exploring Client Concerns

Goal: To distinguish definitions and domains of direct and clinical practice.

Focus Competencies or Practice Behaviors:
- EP 2.1.7a Social workers explore client problems by eliciting comprehensive data.
- EP 2.1.10b Social workers establish rapport and enhance motivation

In chapter 3, ways to introduce contact to clients, explore their concerns and begin to establish rapport are discussed on pages 37 and 38. This is especially important when clients have not sought services. An example for how to explain the offer of service is made based on the video "Hanging with Hailey" (HWH)

1. What are the steps involved in explain the offer of service and options available?

2. Your field agency provides housing services for homeless persons. Priority is given to persons who face multiple barriers such as diagnosed mental illness. Among conditions of the housing service are that recipients of the service must be actively engaged with a helping professional in working on mutually defined issues. In your own words, describe for the client the factors involved in your offer of service.

3. You are placed at a public high school. Clients are often referred to you related to truancy or classroom behavior issues. Should their parents or guardians agree for them to be seen, you can explore concerns and goals as the adolescents see them. You have to make them aware of truancy laws, if that is relevant, but adolescents can otherwise decide whether they wish to accept your services. Describe in your own words how you would make an offer of service.

Exercise 3.2
Physical Conditions for an Interview

Goal: To be aware of favorable conditions for conducting an interview.

Focus Competencies or Practice Behaviors:
- EP 2.1.10a Substantively and affectively prepare for action with individuals, families, groups.

Chapter 3 describes eight conditions that are favorable for conducting an interview. List those conditions and explain how a social worker might use that information to prepare working with a client.

Exercise 3.3
Establishing Rapport

Goal: To explore methods of establishing rapport with clients.

Focus Competencies or Practice Behaviors:
- EP 2.1.10b. Social workers use empathy and other interpersonal skills.

In the video "Hanging with Hailey" (HWH), the social worker makes several efforts to establish rapport with the initially hesitant potential client, Hailey. Describe those efforts. What might you have done differently?

How have you attempted to establish rapport with clients?

Exercise 3.4
Identifying Steps in Helping Process

Goal: To explore various roles performed by social workers in specific case situation

Focus Competencies or Practice Behaviors:
- EP 2.1.10. Social workers engage, assess, intervene and evaluate with individuals families and groups.
- EP 2.1.10k Social workers negotiate, mediate and advocate for clients.

Ali meets with the Corning family in the video "Work with the Corning Family".

1. How does Ali describe functions performed by her agency? What social work roles are performed by the agency?

2. What roles does Ali perform with the Corning family?

3. What benefits can there be for a family if an agency performs multiple social work roles? Can you describe an instance of a family benefiting from multiple functions or roles performed by an agency?

Exercise 3.5
Attending to Concerns and Strengths

Goal: To include attention both to concerns and strengths

Focus Competencies or Practice Behaviors:
- EP 2.1.10f Social workers develop mutually agreed upon intervention goals and objectives.

In chapter 3 we discuss the process of establishing goals with clients. After reading, answer the following questions:

1. What kinds of special knowledge and resources belong to potential clients in determining goals of interventions?

2. What are the potential hazards of ignoring or diminishing the knowledge, resources and desires of potential clients in determining goals of intervention?

3. What might be circumstances in which being guided only by potential client perceived goals might be detrimental in determining goals for intervention?

4. Apply these considerations of the contribution of client and social worker to determining goals of intervention. What factors should be considered? Make a case for how you would choose to proceed.

   a. Jim is in a day treatment program for adult male sex offenders whom are struggling with Serious and Persistent Mental Illness and/or cognitive delays. He is court mandated to participate in the program. Jim attends treatment for 3 hours a day, 5 days a week in a group setting. He also meets with an individual case worker for an hour each week. Jim is very over weight and says that he would like to lose 50 pounds. In the past he has always met women on line. He has been prevented from doing this in the treatment program. He would like to learn safe ways to meet and interact with women.

   b. Robert, 7, is placed in a therapeutic day treatment program mornings while he attends classes in the afternoon. He has low frustration tolerance and has difficulty calming down when upset. His anger escalates within seconds. He cries for long periods of time until he is too weak to walk and at those times he also spits on walls or himself. He believes that no other human being is capable of loving him and when he is given a compliment he receives it negatively. His therapist wants him to work on frustration tolerance, academic anxiety, physical aggression and difficulty calming down. He is asked to try to notice when he is getting stuck and to let individuals around him (especially adults) know what he is doing. He has the tendency to walk out in the middle of conversations or during group sessions. Robert does not like to be touched but sometimes he acts to harm himself and at that point he has to be held. When he takes a break in the break room he damages the walls and the doorknob and has physically assaulted staff multiple times. He spits on the walls and the doors even though he knows he is responsible for cleaning it when he is calmed.

   c. Candace came on her own to a family service clinic. She describes herself as having a negative self-image, depression concerns, and concern about her weight. She feels depressed, doesn't eat in a healthy way and feels a general lack of energy. Otherwise things are fine. She has a good job and makes a comfortable living.

   d. Laura runs a daycare center. She currently has 12 children. Until a month ago, she had 7 children. She has noticed that since the addition of the additional daycare children she has become much more irritable with her own children, and finds herself "snapping" at them, quicker to punish than before, and feeling terrible because of this. She realizes that she is incredibly busy all day with all these children, and that it gets to be a lot of work. She said that she used to be a very patient mother that would sit down and talk to her children about what was going on, and now finds herself yelling at them, and often sending them right to the corner or their bedrooms. She said she does not get upset with the daycare children, just her own children. Tensions are also developing with her husband who is away from the home often on a job requiring extensive commuting. She is very tense, disappointed in herself, and wants to be more calm, to be a better parent and better day care provider. She has contacted a local family agency.

Chapter 3
Competencies/Practice Behaviors Exercises Assessment:

Name: _____   Date: _____

Supervisor's Name: _____

Focus Competencies:
- EP 2.1.7a Social workers explore client problems by eliciting comprehensive data.
- EP 2.1.10. Social workers engage, assess, intervene and evaluate with individuals families and groups.
- EP 2.1.10a substantively and affectively prepare for action with individuals, families, groups, organizations and communities
- EP 2.1.10b Social workers establish rapport and enhance motivation
- EP 2.1.10f Social workers develop mutually agreed upon intervention goals and objectives.
- EP 2.1.10.k social workers negotiate, mediate and advocate for clients.

Instructions: Evaluate your work or your partner's work in the Focus Practice Behaviors by completing the Practice Behaviors Assessment form below. What other Practice Behaviors did you use to complete these Exercises? Be sure to record them in your assessments. Please note that as you are beginning your work in this course, high level attainment of competencies at this point in your program is not anticipated. Over the course of this course and this program, your proficiency should increase to the point that you and other competent assessors will agree that you have attained the competency at a satisfactory level.

1.	I have attained this competency/practice behavior (in the range of 80 to 100%)
2.	I have largely attained this competency/practice behavior (in the range of 60 to 80%)
3.	I have partially attained this competency/practice behavior (in the range of 40 to 60%)
4.	I have made a little progress in attaining this competency/practice behavior (in the range of 20 to 40%
5.	I have made almost no progress in attaining this competency/practice behavior (in the range of 0 to 20%)

EPAS 2008 Core Competencies & Core Practice Behaviors	Student Self Assessment						Evaluator Feedback
Student and Evaluator Assessment Scale and Comments	0	1	2	3	4	5	Agree/Disagree/Comments
EP 2.1.1 Identify as a Professional Social Worker and Conduct Oneself Accordingly							
a. Advocate for client access to the services of social work							
b. Practice personal reflection and self-correction to assure continual professional development							

c. Attend to professional roles and boundaries							
d. Demonstrate professional demeanor in behavior, appearance, and communication							
e. Engage in career-long learning							
f. Use supervision and consultation							
EP 2.1.2 Apply Social Work Ethical Principles to Guide Professional Practice							
a. Recognize and manage personal values in a way that allows professional values to guide practice							
b. Make ethical decisions by applying NASW Code of Ethics and, as applicable, of the IFSW/IASSW Ethics in Social Work, Statement of Principles							
c. Tolerate ambiguity in resolving ethical conflicts							
d. Apply strategies of ethical reasoning to arrive at principled decisions							
EP 2.1.3 Apply Critical Thinking to Inform and Communicate Professional Judgments							
a. Distinguish, appraise, and integrate multiple sources of knowledge, including research-based knowledge and practice wisdom							
b. Analyze models of assessment, prevention, intervention, and evaluation							
c. Demonstrate effective oral and written communication in working with individuals, families, groups, organizations, communities, and colleagues							
EP 2.1.4 Engage Diversity and Difference in Practice							
a. Recognize the extent to which a culture's structures and values may oppress,							

marginalize, alienate, or create or enhance privilege and power							
b. Gain sufficient self-awareness to eliminate the influence of personal biases and values in working with diverse groups							
c. Recognize and communicate their understanding of the importance of difference in shaping life experiences							
d. View themselves as learners and engage those with whom they work as informants							
EP 2.1.5 Advance Human Rights and Social and Economic Justice							
a. Understand forms and mechanisms of oppression and discrimination							
b. Advocate for human rights and social and economic justice							
c. Engage in practices that advance social and economic justice							
EP 2.1.6 Engage in Research-Informed Practice and Practice-Informed Research							
a. Use practice experience to inform scientific inquiry							
b. Use research evidence to inform practice							
EP 2.1.7 Apply Knowledge of Human Behavior and the Social Environment							
a. Utilize conceptual frameworks to guide the processes of assessment, intervention, and evaluation							
b. Critique and apply knowledge to understand person and environment							
EP 2.1.8 Engage in Policy Practice to Advance Social and Economic Well-Being and to Deliver Effective Social Work Services							
a. Analyze, formulate, and advocate for policies that advance social well-being							
b. Collaborate with colleagues and clients for effective policy action							

EP 2.1.9 Respond to Contexts that Shape Practice							
a. Continuously discover, appraise, and attend to changing locales, populations, scientific and technological developments, and emerging societal trends to provide relevant services							
b. Provide leadership in promoting sustainable changes in service delivery and practice to improve the quality of social services							
EP 2.1.10 Engage, Assess, Intervene, and Evaluate with Individuals, Families, Groups, Organizations and Communities							
a. Substantively and affectively prepare for action with individuals, families, groups, organizations, and communities							
b. Use empathy and other interpersonal skills							
c. Develop a mutually agreed-on focus of work and desired outcomes							
d. Collect, organize, and interpret client data							
e. Assess client strengths and limitations							
f. Develop mutually agreed-on intervention goals and objectives							
g. Select appropriate intervention strategies							
h. Initiate actions to achieve organizational goals							
i. Implement prevention interventions that enhance client capacities							
j. Help clients resolve problems							
k. Negotiate, mediate, and advocate for clients							
l. Facilitate transitions and endings							
m. Critically analyze, monitor, and evaluate interventions							

Chapter 4
Operationalizing the Cardinal Social Work Values

Exercise 4.1
What Pushes My Buttons?

Goal: To develop insight into value conflicts, countertransference, and emotional reactions that can arise in social work practice.

Focus Competencies or Practice Behaviors:
- EP 2.1.1.b Practice personal reflection and self-correction to assure continual professional development
- EP 2.1.1.c Attend to professional roles and boundaries
- EP 2.1.1.d Demonstrate professional demeanor in behavior, appearance, and communication
- EP 2.1.1.f Use supervision and consultation
- EP 2.1.2.a Recognize and manage personal values in a way that allows professional values to guide practice
- EP 2.1.10.a Substantively and affectively prepare for action with individuals, families, groups, organizations, and communities

Instructions:

1. Rate each of the following vignettes on the following scale to reflect your reaction to the case: 1) Strong negative reaction 2) Mild negative reaction 3) Mild positive reaction, 4) Mild positive reaction.

2. Identify the values, beliefs and/or feelings associated with your reaction.

3. Identify the effects your reaction might have on your service in each case.

4. Describe the steps you will take to address these reactions and uphold your professional responsibilities.

At the conclusion of the written exercise, the instructor can facilitate paired or whole group discussion of the vignettes and offer suggestions for identifying and managing strong reactions to case scenarios.

Vignette A

You are working with a family in which the 15-year-old is expected to quit after-school sports and activities so that she can help babysit for her 17-year-old sister's infant.

1   2   3   4

Effects of my reactions:

Steps to address my reactions:

Vignette B

You are coordinating a holiday gift donation program at a school. When the students open their presents, many toss them aside and shout in disgust because the items are used or out-dated.

1   2   3   4

Effects of my reactions:

Steps to address my reactions

Vignette C

Your client is having financial difficulties affecting her children but she always has elaborate hairstyles and manicured nail designs.

1   2   3   4

Effects of my reactions:

Steps to address my reactions:

Vignette D

A family with limited finances has children with asthma who require frequent visits to the emergency room. They have several cats and large dogs that they say are "like family".

1   2   3   4

Effects of my reactions:

Steps to address my reactions:

Vignette E

A woman whose husband broke her collarbone with a chair has decided to leave the shelter and return to him because he "felt awful about what he did and promised to change".

1   2   3   4

Effects of my reactions

Steps to address my reactions

Vignette F

Your client has five daughters ages 7 and under, three of whom have severe physical and cognitive impairments. The client has just told you she is pregnant again, "hoping for a boy."

1   2   3   4

Effects of my reactions

Steps to address my reactions

Vignette G

Your new client is a male dressed as a woman.

1   2   3   4

Effects of my reactions

Steps to address my reactions

Vignette H
Your client complains that he can't find a job but plays video games all day.

1   2   3   4

Effects of my reactions

Steps to address my reactions

Vignette H
You are working with a recently discharged injured veteran whose spouse asked for a divorce while the service member was in the hospital.

1   2   3   4

Effects of my reactions

Steps to address my reactions

Exercise 4.2
Telling Right from Wrong

Goal: To differentiate between ethical, unethical, and ambiguous professional behaviors.

Focus Competencies or Practice Behaviors:
- EP 2.1.1.b Practice personal reflection and self-correction to assure continual professional development
- EP 2.1.1.c Attend to professional roles and boundaries
- EP 2.1.2.a Recognize and manage personal values in a way that allows professional values to guide practice
- EP 2.1.2.b Make ethical decisions by applying standards of the National Association of Social Workers Code of Ethics and, as applicable, of the International Federation of Social Workers/International Association of Schools of Social Work Ethics in Social Work, Statement of Principles
- EP 2.1.2.c Tolerate ambiguity in resolving ethical conflicts
- EP 2.1.2.d Apply strategies of ethical reasoning to arrive at principled decisions
- EP 2.1.10.a Substantively and affectively prepare for action with individuals, families, groups, organizations, and communities

Instructions:

For each case indicate whether, according to social work values and ethical standards, the action is ethical or unethical. If you think the answer may depend on certain situational factors, note them in the space provided.

The instructor can facilitate paired or whole group discussion of the findings and provide feedback on the choices class members selected.

Case 1: The social worker asked the client to become a sales person in the worker's vitamin sales business.

__ Ethical

__ Unethical

__ It depends on:

Case 2: A social worker shared a beer with a client during a home visit in an effort to build rapport.

__ Ethical

__ Unethical

__ It depends on:

Case 3: A school social worker gave her son's used clothes to a boy on her caseload.

__ Ethical

__ Unethical

__ It depends on:

Case 4: A social worker asked to have a case transferred when she realized the client was a close friend of her mother's.

__ Ethical

__ Unethical

__ It depends on:

Case 5: A client works at the local sports arena. The social worker asked if the client could help get tickets, even though the game is sold out. The worker intends to pay for the tickets.

__ Ethical

__ Unethical

__ It depends on:

Case 6: The social worker has to miss a family reunion because she might be called to testify in court on a high profile case. The case is in the news, so she is comfortable letting her mother know this is the one she is working on instead of joining the family gathering.

__ Ethical

__ Unethical

__ It depends on:

Case 7: The social worker and client are in the same bible study group at church.

__ Ethical

__ Unethical

__ It depends on:

Case 8: The social worker promises the client that everything said in their meetings will be confidential. The worker feels that without this promise, the client won't discuss anything meaningful.

__ Ethical

__ Unethical

__ It depends on:

Case 9: The social worker and client have lunch together.

__ Ethical

__ Unethical

__ It depends on:

Case 10: The social worker offers to babysit for the client's children while she is at a job interview.

__ Ethical

__ Unethical

__ It depends on:

Case 11: The social worker offers to hug the client.

__ Ethical

__ Unethical

__ It depends on:

Case 12: An agency hires a former client in a clerical position.

__ Ethical

__ Unethical

__ It depends on:

Goal: To identify the ways that personal characteristics can impinge on professional behaviors.

Focus Competencies or Practice Behaviors:
- EP 2.1.1.b Practice personal reflection and self-correction to assure continual professional development
- EP 2.1.1.c Attend to professional roles and boundaries
- EP 2.1.2.a Recognize and manage personal values in a way that allows professional values to guide practice
- EP 2.1.10.a Substantively and affectively prepare for action with individuals, families, groups, organizations, and communities

This exercise is intended to help you identify the ways the personal needs and interests can become assets or deficits in social work practice. For each item below, identify the ways that that characteristic can enhance professional practice and the ways that it can become a deterrent.

Following the assignment, the instructor may facilitate discussion on the findings and on strategies for being aware of personal needs or characteristics and the implications for social work practice.

Personal Quality/ Characteristic	Advantages for Social Work Practice	Disadvantages for Social Work Practice
Need to be liked		
Perfectionist		
Has personal experience with trauma or social problems		
Eager to create change		
Efficient		
Easygoing		

Afraid of making mistakes		
Witty		
Dislikes conflict		
Wants to make a difference		
Accepting of others		
Organized		

Exercise 4.4
What Would You Do?

Goal: Gain deeper awareness of personal values, professional roles, and ethical decision making.

Focus Competencies or Practice Behaviors:
- EP 2.1.1.b Practice personal reflection and self-correction to assure continual professional development
- EP 2.1.1.c Attend to professional roles and boundaries
- EP 2.1.2.a Recognize and manage personal values in a way that allows professional values to guide practice
- EP 2.1.2.b Make ethical decisions by applying standards of the National Association of Social Workers Code of Ethics and, as applicable, of the International Federation of Social Workers/International Association of Schools of Social Work Ethics in Social Work, Statement of Principles
- EP 2.1.2.c Tolerate ambiguity in resolving ethical conflicts
- EP 2.1.2.d Apply strategies of ethical reasoning to arrive at principled decisions
- EP 2.1.10.a Substantively and affectively prepare for action with individuals, families, groups, organizations, and communities

Following the prompts, indicate what you would do in the situation described and the basis for your decision.

The instructor may continue the exercise by facilitating a discussion about various choices made by class members. As you hear various reactions, do you find some that conflict with your response? Do any make you reconsider your response in favor of a better option? Do any raise ethical concerns themselves?

- 35 -

What would you do if...

1....you were visiting a client's home and he/she offered you a piece of cake?

Response:

Rationale:

2. ...you went to see a patient at the hospital and found the person you were sent to visit is someone you know?

Response:

Rationale:

3...a client invited you to her baby shower?

Response:

Rationale:

4. ...your co-workers discussed cases in the elevator and in other non-private places?

Response:

Rationale:

5. ...an elderly client told you she intended to leave you in her will?

Response:

Rationale:

6. …your roommate asked if you knew anything about a case (one that you are actually working on)?

Response:

Rationale:

7. …you were enjoying an icy beer at a jazz festival with your partner when a client sat nearby, looked up and noticed you?

Response:

Rationale:

8. …a senior supervisor at another agency called to ask you about services for a client. You do not know if a confidentiality waiver has been signed.

Response:

Rationale:

Exercise 4.5
Ethical Decision Making

Goal: To practice use of an ethical decision making model.

Focus Competencies or Practice Behaviors:
- EP 2.1.1.b Practice personal reflection and self-correction to assure continual professional development
- EP 2.1.1.f Use supervision and consultation
- EP 2.1.2.a Recognize and manage personal values in a way that allows professional values to guide practice
- EP 2.1.2.b Make ethical decisions by applying standards of the National Association of Social Workers Code of Ethics and, as applicable, of the International Federation of Social Workers/International Association of Schools of Social Work Ethics in Social Work, Statement of Principles
- EP 2.1.2.c Tolerate ambiguity in resolving ethical conflicts
- EP 2.1.2.d Apply strategies of ethical reasoning to arrive at principled decisions
- EP 2.1.10.a Substantively and affectively prepare for action with individuals, families, groups, organizations, and communities

Using one or more of the following cases, the class should engage in whole group discussion of the dilemma presented, using the following steps adapted from Chapter 4. Alternatively, the instructor may break the class into small groups and assign each group to answer one of the steps then bring them together to compile the results, weigh the options, and arrive at a decision. The class should then engage in a whole-group discussion of the strategies to effectively *carry out* the decision and the ways that the effectiveness of the decision could be evaluated.

1. What is the problem or dilemma? (Gather as much information about the situation from as many perspectives as possible, including that of the client).

2. What core principles and the competing issues are imbedded in the case?

3. What do Codes of Ethics suggest for responding to the case?

4. What laws, policies, and regulations apply to the case?

5. Who should the social worker(s) consult with in resolving the dilemma?

6. What are the possible and probable courses of action? What are the consequences of various options?

Case One
Clients at the ABC agency are required to go attend parenting workshops at another agency as part of their service plans for family reunification. The leaders of the parenting workshops are ineffective in improving parenting and disrespectful toward the participants, but ABC must refer clients there because but that's who the funder chose to subcontract with as the result of a low bid.

Case Two

While the social worker is in the family's home, doing a developmental assessment on the toddler, he/she notices the family dog is chained to a tree without shade and water. The dog looks undernourished and howls pitifully when the worker walks to the house.

Case Three

The state adoption agency uses the internet and events like picnics and talent shows to advertise children who are available for adoption. Some of the children are embarrassed by these experiences and others become anxious and discouraged when they are not approached by prospective families at events. The adoption agency says that photolisting and family fairs are the most effective ways to recruit prospective families and get children into permanent homes.

Case Four

A state initiative encourages the hiring of mental health consumers at nonprofit agencies, based on the belief that service recipients can serve as valuable peer advisors even while they are still seeking services themselves. One agency is not sure whether this is an ethically sound process and would like your advice.

Case Five

A social worker is assigned to help homeless clients find permanent supportive housing. A client who is on the sex offender registry just moved into an apartment building where the social worker's sister and children live.

Role Play Exercise 4.6 **Informed Consent**

Goal: To help students develop skills comfort in addressing informed consent

Focus Competencies or Practice Behaviors:
- EP 2.1.1.d Demonstrate professional demeanor in behavior, appearance, and communication
- EP 2.1.1.f Use supervision and consultation
- EP 2.1.2.b Make ethical decisions by applying standards of the National Association of Social Workers Code of Ethics and, as applicable, of the International Federation of Social Workers/International Association of Schools of Social Work Ethics in Social Work, Statement of Principles
- EP 2.1.10.a Substantively and affectively prepare for action with individuals, families, groups, organizations, and communities.

Instructions:

The NASW Code of Ethics states that "social workers should use clear and understandable language to inform clients of the purpose of the services, risks related to the services, limits to services because of the requirements of a third-party payer, relevant costs, reasonable alternatives, clients' right to refuse or withdraw consent, and the time frame covered by the consent. Social workers should provide clients with an opportunity to ask questions"

(NASW, 2008, pp. 7-8). Common topics for informed consent at the beginning of service include the social worker's credentials (or student status), limits on confidentiality, and agency policies.

The discussion of informed consent can be difficult because it typically comes first at the outset of service, when the worker and client are strangers and when both are eager to begin addressing the client's needs. Informed consent can also be shortchanged because professionals are uncomfortable with information they are sharing and thus are tempted to skim over parts that might upset, offend, or shut down the client. Practicing the discussion of informed consent will increase skill and comfort with the process.

1. Break into groups of three.

2. Each group member should take turns as the client, social worker, and observer

3. The "social worker" should introduce the ground rules of service, using the information above or in Chapter 4 as a guide. The "client" should react, employing a common response (passive agreement, impatience, suspicion, confusion, questions, etc.), to which the "social worker" should then respond. When the client has given verbal consent for service, the role play is over.

4. The observer shares feedback on the strengths and weaknesses that the social worker displayed. The group discusses reactions to the role play and ideas for improving future informed consent discussions.

5. Steps 3 and 4 are repeated until all group members have had the opportunity to portray the social worker.

6. The instructor solicits examples from the class of a particularly effective example of informed consent and that student demonstrates through role play for the class.

Chapter 4
Competencies/Practice Behaviors Exercises Assessment:

Name: _____ Date: _____

Supervisor's Name: _____

Focus Competencies/Practice Behaviors:

- EP 2.1.1.b Practice personal reflection and self-correction to assure continual professional development
- EP 2.1.1.c Attend to professional roles and boundaries
- EP 2.1.1.d Demonstrate professional demeanor in behavior, appearance, and communication
- EP 2.1.1.f Use supervision and consultation
- EP 2.1.2.a Recognize and manage personal values in a way that allows professional values to guide practice
- EP 2.1.2.b Make ethical decisions by applying standards of the National Association of Social Workers Code of Ethics and, as applicable, of the International Federation of Social Workers/International Association of Schools of Social Work Ethics in Social Work, Statement of Principles
- EP 2.1.2.c Tolerate ambiguity in resolving ethical conflicts
- EP 2.1.2.d Apply strategies of ethical reasoning to arrive at principled decisions
- EP 2.1.10.a Substantively and affectively prepare for action with individuals, families, groups, organizations, and communities
- for action with individuals, families, groups, organizations, and communities

Instructions: Evaluate your work or your partner's work in the Focus Practice Behaviors by completing the Practice Behaviors Assessment form below. What other Practice Behaviors did you use to complete these Exercises? Be sure to record them in your assessments.

1.	I have attained this competency/practice behavior (in the range of 80 to 100%)
2.	I have largely attained this competency/practice behavior (in the range of 60 to 80%)
3.	I have partially attained this competency/practice behavior (in the range of 40 to 60%)
4.	I have made a little progress in attaining this competency/practice behavior (in the range of 20 to 40%
5.	I have made almost no progress in attaining this competency/practice behavior (in the range of 0 to 20%)

EPAS 2008 Core Competencies & Core Practice Behaviors	Student Self Assessment						Evaluator Feedback
Student and Evaluator Assessment Scale and Comments	0	1	2	3	4	5	Agree/Disagree/Comments
2.1.1 Identity as a Professional Social Worker and Conduct Oneself Accordingly:							
a. Advocate for client access to the services of social work							
b. Practice personal reflection and self-correction to assure continual professional development							
c. Attend to professional roles and boundaries							

d. Demonstrate professional demeanor in behavior, appearance, and communication								
e. Engage in career-long learning								
f. Use supervision and consultation								
2.1.2 Apply Social Work Ethical Principles to Guide Professional Practice:								
a. Recognize and manage personal values in a way that allows professional values to guide practice								
b. Make ethical decisions by applying NASW Code of Ethics and, as applicable, IFSW/IASSW Ethics in Social Work, Statement of Principles								
c. Tolerate ambiguity in resolving ethical conflicts								
d. Apply strategies in resolving ethical conflicts								
2.1.3 Apply Critical Thinking to Inform and Communicate Professional Judgments:								
a. Distinguish, appraise, and integrate multiple sources of knowledge, including research-based knowledge and practice wisdom								
b. Analyze models of assessment, prevention, intervention, and evaluation								
c. Demonstrate effective oral and written communication in working with individuals, families, groups, organizations, communities, and colleagues								
2.1.4 Engage Diversity and Difference in Practice:								
a. Recognize the extent to which a culture's structures and values may oppress, marginalize, alienate, or create or enhance privilege and power								
b. Gain sufficient self-awareness to eliminate the influence of personal biases and values in working with diverse groups								
c. Recognize and communicate their understanding of the importance of difference in shaping life experiences								

d. View themselves as learners and engage those with whom they work as informants							

2.1.5 Advance Human Rights and Social and Economic Justice

a. Understand forms and mechanisms of oppression and discrimination							
b. Advocate for human rights and social and economic justice							
c. Engage in practices that advance social and economic justice							

2.1.6 Engage in research-informed practice and practice-informed research

a. Use practice experience to inform scientific inquiry							
b. Use research evidence to inform practice							

2.1.7 Apply knowledge of human behavior and the social environment:

a. Utilize conceptual frameworks to guide the processes of assessment, intervention, and evaluation							
b. Critique and apply knowledge to understand person and environment							

2.1.8 Engage in policy practice to advance social and economic well-being and to deliver effective social work services:

a. Analyze, formulate, and advocate for policies that advance social well-being							
b. Collaborate with colleagues and clients for effective policy action							

2.1.9 Respond to contexts that shape practice:

a. Continuously discover, appraise, and attend to changing locales, populations, scientific and technological developments, and emerging societal trends to provide relevant services							
b. Provide leadership in promoting sustainable changes in service delivery and practice to improve the quality of social services							

2.1.10 Engage, assess, intervene, and evaluate with individuals, families, groups, organizations and communities:

a. Substantively and affectively prepare for action with individuals, families, groups, organizations, and communities							
b. Use empathy and other interpersonal skills							

c. Develop a mutually agreed-on focus of work and desired outcomes							
d. Collect, organize, and interpret client data							
e. Assess client strengths and limitations							
f. Develop mutually agreed-on intervention goals and objectives							
g. Select appropriate intervention strategies.							
h. Initiate actions to achieve organizational goals							
i. Implement prevention interventions that enhance client capacities							
j. Help clients resolve problems							
k. Negotiate, mediate, and advocate for clients							
l. Facilitate transitions and endings							
m. Critically analyze, monitor, and evaluate interventions							

Exercise 5.1
Goal: Show that You Have Heard

Goal: Responding with Empathy.

Focus Competencies or Practice Behaviors:
- EP 2.1.10 Engage, assess, intervene, and evaluate with individuals, families, groups, organizations and communities.
- EP 2.1.10a Substantively and affectively prepare for action with individuals, families, groups, organizations, and communities
- EP 2.1.10b Use empathy and other interpersonal skills

Chapter 5 contains many examples of client messages and models of empathic responses. You can now try to respond with a level 3 empathic response that can be a reasonable goal for communication in a first session. Read the client message and compose an empathic response that captures the client's surface feelings. You can later have a partner read the situation to you and you can practice a verbal response. You may want to use the paradigm"You feel ___ about (or because) ___," in organizing your response before phrasing it in typical conversation language. Strive to make your responses fresh, varied, and spontaneous. To expand your repertoire of responses, we strongly encourage you to continue using the lists of affective words and phrases.

1. Maureen says that she has been sober now for 4 years and now feels eager to see if she can get into a new relationship that might be safe for her. She is somewhat fearful because her previous relationship when not sober was abusive.

2. Mrs. Roberts was divorced a year ago and is concerned about the effect on her daughter Clarice, 12, who sometimes vents saying "I hate you! I wish you weren't my mother!" Clarice has also said "I hate myself, I wish I wasn't born" and "I'm a bad person."

3. You are a part of a county children's crisis response team. You responded to a frantic mother stating that her son was "out of control." Upon arrival the client (Charles, 15) was chasing his mother around the house with a machete. The police were called and John was placed in the county JDC. When you meet with Charles, he says that he does not like living with his mother, who is divorced from his father. Charles' family

is Hmong and typically when there is a separation, male children go with the father and his clan. In this case, however, Charles could not be controlled by his father so he had to move. Charles says he has no friends in the new school, and that his mother and he have different religions: she is a Christian and he is an Animist. He wants to be respected and not pestered all the time.

4. Darius recently graduated from college and has been experiencing some anxiety about getting a job. He reports procrastinating about following up on applications, interviews and opportunities for employment. He says that he sits, worries and frets that "they aren't calling". Often he then becomes frustrated and decides he is no long interested in the position or living arrangement instead of calling and contacting them and inquiring. He wonders whether getting a degree was all worth it.

Exercise 5.2
When It is Hard to Be Empathic

Goal: To be aware of favorable conditions for conducting an interview.

Focus Competencies or Practice Behaviors:
- EP 2.1.10a Substantively and affectively prepare for action with individuals, families, groups.
- EP 2.1.10b Use empathy and other interpersonal skills

Some of the above situations about conveying empathy may have stimulated conflicting emotions in you. Remember that conveying empathy does not mean that you condone the client's behavior or thoughts. Clients need to feel understood before they can address the consequences of their behavior and choices.

1. If you were to work with Maureen, what aspects of her story would make it easier to convey empathy to her?

2. What aspects would make it more difficult for you?

3. What could you do about those aspects which made it more difficult?

4. If you were to work with Mrs. Roberts, what aspects of her story would make it easier to convey empathy to her?

- 46 -

5. What aspects would make it more difficult for you?

6. What could you do about those aspects which made it more difficult?

7. If you were to work with Charles, what aspects of her story would make it easier to convey empathy to him?

8. What aspects would make it more difficult for you?

9. What could you do about those aspects which made it more difficult?

10. If you were to work with Darius, what aspects of his story would make it easier to convey empathy to him?

11. What aspects would make it more difficult for you?

12. What could you do about those aspects which made it more difficult?

Exercise 5.3
Measuring Empathy

Goal: To explore methods of establishing rapport with clients. .

Focus Competencies or Practice Behaviors:
- EP 2.1.10b. Social workers use empathy and other interpersonal skills. .

The videos that are available with this book provide a rich source for assessing efforts at conveying empathy.

1. In the video "Domestic Violence and the Probation Officer: I" assess the communication in terms of levels of empathy. Write an example of any level of empathy that you observe:

   a. Level 0 or 1:

   b. Level 2:

c. Level 3:

d. Level 4:

e. Level 5:

2. Now, assess the video "Domestic Violence and the Probation Officer: II. As before, assess the communication in terms of levels of empathy. Write an example of any level of empathy that you observe:

a. Level 0 or 1:

b. Level 2:

c. Level 3:

d. Level 4:

e. Level 5:

3. Now pick any other video associated with this text or observe an interview with a fellow student. Assess the communication in terms of levels of empathy. Write an example of any level of empathy that you observe:

a. Level 0 or 1:

b. Level 2:

c. Level 3:

d. Level 4:

e. Level 5:

Exercise 5.4
Practicing Firm Requests

Goal: To practice making a firm request

Focus Competencies or Practice Behaviors:
- EP 2.1.10b. Social workers use empathy and other interpersonal skills.

In Chapter 5, the process of making firm requests is discussed. Note that sometimes individuals and families can be assisted by altering the process of the session. For each situation below, practice making a firm request.

1. As family members are asked to describe what brought them in to meet with you, several start to talk at once, talking over one another.

2. In meeting with a single parent father and adolescent son, the father, Mr. Davis, begins to recite chapter and verse how disappointed he is in his son Ralph. He feels that he never had the opportunities that Ralph has and he is squandering them. Meanwhile Ralph is texting with this cell phone and mumbling "whatever."

Goal: To practice responding authentically

Focus Competencies or Practice Behaviors:
- EP 2.1.10b. Social workers use empathy and other interpersonal skills.

Guidelines for responding authentically were discussed in your readings. Take each of the following situations and formulate an authentic response.

1. Your 15-year-old client Marsha is doing very well academically in school but has had considerable conflict with her family because she is dating an older male who has dropped out of school and who is ethnically different from her. She has just shared with you that she has figured out the solution to her situation. She will get pregnant by Rory, her boyfriend, and then she will move out and raise this child on her own or with Rory. She knows that she could be a better parent than either one she has had.

2. Your client is a young single parent in an independent living program. The program strives to support young men and women toward independence. Your client has requested your personal cell phone number to call if she becomes lonely during your time off. Boundaries have been varied in this program across several workers.

3. You are a part of a community support program that works with Karl, a 25-year-old man with a serious and persistent illness. Karl reports that he has few friends or social supports. He is often bored which tempts him to use, and overuse, alcohol. Karl says that he "lost" most of his friends when he was first hospitalized. He attends a dual-diagnosis treatment group through Shady Haven Resources once a week, and while he enjoys attending the group and connecting with the other members, he has not gotten together with anyone outside of the group. Karl says he likes you very much and would like to be your friend, to do some friend type things together.

Chapter 5
Competencies/Practice Behaviors Exercises Assessment:

Name: _____ Date: _____

Supervisor's Name: _____

Focus Competencies:
- EP 2.1.10a Substantively and affectively prepare for action with individuals, families, groups.
- EP 2.1.10b Social workers establish rapport and enhance motivation

Instructions: Evaluate your work or your partner's work in the Focus Practice Behaviors by completing the Practice Behaviors Assessment form below. What other Practice Behaviors did you use to complete these Exercises? Be sure to record them in your assessments. Please note that as you are beginning your work in this course, high level attainment of competencies at this point in your program is not anticipated. Over the course of this course and this program, your proficiency should increase to the point that you and other competent assessors will agree that you have attained the competency at a satisfactory level.

1.	I have attained this competency/practice behavior (in the range of 80 to 100%)
2.	I have largely attained this competency/practice behavior (in the range of 60 to 80%)
3.	I have partially attained this competency/practice behavior (in the range of 40 to 60%)
4.	I have made a little progress in attaining this competency/practice behavior (in the range of 20 to 40%
5.	I have made almost no progress in attaining this competency/practice behavior (in the range of 0 to 20%)

EPAS 2008 Core Competencies & Core Practice Behaviors	Student Self Assessment						Evaluator Feedback
Student and Evaluator Assessment Scale and Comments	0	1	2	3	4	5	Agree/Disagree/Comments
EP 2.1.1 Identify as a Professional Social Worker and Conduct Oneself Accordingly							
a. Advocate for client access to the services of social work							
b. Practice personal reflection and self-correction to assure continual professional development							
c. Attend to professional roles and boundaries							
d. Demonstrate professional demeanor in behavior, appearance, and communication							
e. Engage in career-long learning							
f. Use supervision and consultation							

EP 2.1.2 Apply Social Work Ethical Principles to Guide Professional Practice							
a. Recognize and manage personal values in a way that allows professional values to guide practice							
b. Make ethical decisions by applying NASW Code of Ethics and, as applicable, of the IFSW/IASSW Ethics in Social Work, Statement of Principles							
c. Tolerate ambiguity in resolving ethical conflicts							
d. Apply strategies of ethical reasoning to arrive at principled decisions							
EP 2.1.3 Apply Critical Thinking to Inform and Communicate Professional Judgments							
a. Distinguish, appraise, and integrate multiple sources of knowledge, including research-based knowledge and practice wisdom							
b. Analyze models of assessment, prevention, intervention, and evaluation							
c. Demonstrate effective oral and written communication in working with individuals, families, groups, organizations, communities, and colleagues							
EP 2.1.4 Engage Diversity and Difference in Practice							
a. Recognize the extent to which a culture's structures and values may oppress, marginalize, alienate, or create or enhance privilege and power							
b. Gain sufficient self-awareness to eliminate the influence of personal biases and values in working with diverse groups							

c. Recognize and communicate their understanding of the importance of difference in shaping life experiences								
d. View themselves as learners and engage those with whom they work as informants								
EP 2.1.5 Advance Human Rights and Social and Economic Justice								
a. Understand forms and mechanisms of oppression and discrimination								
b. Advocate for human rights and social and economic justice								
c. Engage in practices that advance social and economic justice								
EP 2.1.6 Engage in Research-Informed Practice and Practice-Informed Research								
a. Use practice experience to inform scientific inquiry								
b. Use research evidence to inform practice								
EP 2.1.7 Apply Knowledge of Human Behavior and the Social Environment								
a. Utilize conceptual frameworks to guide the processes of assessment, intervention, and evaluation								
b. Critique and apply knowledge to understand person and environment								
EP 2.1.8 Engage in Policy Practice to Advance Social and Economic Well-Being and to Deliver Effective Social Work Services								
a. Analyze, formulate, and advocate for policies that advance social well-being								
b. Collaborate with colleagues and clients for effective policy action								
EP 2.1.9 Respond to Contexts that Shape Practice								
a. Continuously discover, appraise, and attend to changing locales, populations, scientific and technological developments, and emerging societal trends to provide relevant services								

b. Provide leadership in promoting sustainable changes in service delivery and practice to improve the quality of social services							
EP 2.1.10 Engage, Assess, Intervene, and Evaluate with Individuals, Families, Groups, Organizations and Communities							
a. Substantively and affectively prepare for action with individuals, families, groups, organizations, and communities							
b. Use empathy and other interpersonal skills							
c. Develop a mutually agreed-on focus of work and desired outcomes							
d. Collect, organize, and interpret client data							
e. Assess client strengths and limitations							
f. Develop mutually agreed-on intervention goals and objectives							
g. Select appropriate intervention strategies							
h. Initiate actions to achieve organizational goals							
i. Implement prevention interventions that enhance client capacities							
j. Help clients resolve problems							
k. Negotiate, mediate, and advocate for clients							
l. Facilitate transitions and endings							
m. Critically analyze, monitor, and evaluate interventions							

Exercise 6.1
Paraphrasing

Goal: Show that You Can Paraphrase the Meaning of What You Have Heard

Focus Competencies or Practice Behaviors:

- EP 2.1.4c Recognize and communicate their understanding of the importance of difference in shaping life experiences
- EP 2.1.4d View themselves as learners and engage those with whom they work as informants
- EP 2.1.10a Substantively and affectively prepare for action with individuals, families, groups, organizations, and communities
- EP 2.1.10b Use empathy and other interpersonal skills

The processes of carrying out an appropriate paraphrase are described in Chapter 6. For each of the following situations, construct an appropriate paraphrase of the meaning of the person's expression.

1. Consumer with a Serious and Persistent Mental Illness (SPMI): " I know I said I would try to get out more and go to the support program but it has been cold and I just have not felt like doing it. I am not sure I would have felt better if I had gone."

2. Client whose partner has left her and is now moving back with her parents temporarily before looking for an apartment on her own: " I just feel like I am starting over again. I thought I had moved out from my parents for good and now I am back with them. I know it makes sense because we can't keep the house and I won't be there long before I find an apartment. It still seems like I am going backwards."

3. Client in first session of Domestic Violence Treatment Program: "I just don't think that all this was my fault. I am a good provider and I should be able to go out with the guys occasionally before I come home."

4. Hispanic single female client is referred to Employee Assistance Program: "I had a breast tumor but it was benign. My mother is getting to a point where she may not be able to live alone and may have to come live here with me. And I am not getting any younger; I want to get married and have some kids before it is too late. So yes, I have a lot going on."

5. Client who has been out of the job market for years :" I mean, figuring out what kind of job I want, that just seems like, so, you know, huge. I don't know where to start."

Exercise 6.2
Complex Reflections

Goal : To be able to carry out complex reflections

Focus Competencies or Practice Behaviors:

- EP 2.1.4c Recognize and communicate their understanding of the importance of difference in shaping life experiences
- EP 2.1.4d View themselves as learners and engage those with whom they work as informants
- EP 2.1.10a Substantively and affectively prepare for action with individuals, families, groups, organizations, and communities
- EP 2.1.10b Use empathy and other interpersonal skills

For each of the following situations, construct an appropriate complex reflection that conveys your understanding of two messages the client is conveying. Note that these are sometimes opposing messages, signaling a conflict that may be contributing to ambivalence about acting. With the following situations, practice complex reflections in which you notice more than one message, including some opposing messages.

1. Client has completed an in-patient treatment program and been prescribed medication. She is also starting school now. "Yeah, I'm hoping that this medication will help me focus a little bit more because I'm kind of all over the place. I'll start something and finish it in a really weird way or not finish it at all. But, I think school will be good for me. I'm not really sure right now, I'm just taking it step-by-step right now." Attempt a complex reflection that recognizes more than one message the client shares.

2. Client is in financial difficulty because of late fees: "Last summer I had this nauseating pain all the time so that I was not keeping up with things. Some bills didn't get paid and now I have all these late fees. It just feels like I can never get ahead and sometimes I just feel like, what's the use, maybe I should just give up."

3. Client has emphysema and has just met with his doctor. The doctor has recommended that he stop smoking." So the doctor says I won't last long unless I quit smoking. But I have been smoking since I was 14 years old. I have tried to stop lots of times but it never lasted."

4. Client in foster care where kinship care was not utilized "All my uncles and other relatives are just slackers. They want someone to take care of them. They can't take care of me. I have been better off in foster care."

    a. What are the consequences of agreeing with a client's negative observation about others?
    b. What alternatives do you have?

5. Client is talking about difficulties in her housing placement where the manager has threatened to evict her "You know, she, [the manager] is a lost cause. I am to the point where they can do whatever they want over there, I am going to move. It's to the point where my kids can't even go outside. I just get so disgusted and irritated that I think any place would be better than here, maybe even being back on the street".

6. Client in domestic violence program: "The reason I am here is my wife was ragging on me all the time. If she had just kept her trap shut and minded her own business, I would not be here. But I guess that now that I am here, I will make the best of it."

    a. As above, what might be the consequence of reflecting directly what the client has said?
    b. What alternatives do you have?

7. Did any of the above situations push your buttons? Which ones? How do you respond when your buttons are pushed? What alternatives do you have when you find yourself responding strongly to client expressions?

Exercise 6.3
Seeking Concreteness

Goal: To be able to obtain specific details in order to better understand what clients are dealing with.

Focus Competencies or Practice Behaviors:

- EP 2.1.10a Substantively and affectively prepare for action with individuals, families, groups.
- EP 2.1.10b Use empathy and other interpersonal skills

Aspects of seeking concreteness are described on pages 144-147 of the 6th chapter. In the following situations, formulate a question that will elicit useful details to aid your understanding.

1. Client reports: "I am really freaked out by my financial situation. I got so many bills, I don't know where to start. Everybody is trying to get a piece of me and I don't have an answer for all of them."

2. Adolescent client has been admitted to the hospital. As a hospital intern, you have asked the client what led he or she to be admitted, the client says "cutting".

3. College student client has come to student clinic reporting anxiety: "I am so behind that I have no chance of passing. I have missed some assignments and turned others in late. I have never done this before."

4. Adolescent at shelter reporting circumstances leading to running away. "My parents freaked out when they found I had a little weed in my back pack. I just said later for all this."

5. Parent of above adolescent when arriving at shelter. "Kids today have no respect. They do things that we would never do in our parents' home."

Exercise 6.4
Summarizing and Focusing

Goal: To summarize what you have heard and help clients focus their expression in order to provide more specific assistance. .

Focus Competencies or Practice Behaviors:
- EP 2.1.10a Substantively and affectively prepare for action with individuals, families, groups.
- EP 2.1.10b Use empathy and other interpersonal skills

How to assist clients in focusing is described on pages 151-154 of the 6th chapter. In the following situations, formulate a response that will assist clients in focusing. Note that an empathizing and summarizing statement presented first can assist clients in feeling heard before you proceed to focus.

1. Client at homeless shelter as part of intake reports: "I have got all these things happening at once. I have to get the kids enrolled in school. I need to get a replacement medical card. I got to apply for work. And I have to comply with anything you need to qualify for the shelter

2. Senior client suffering from a physical condition in her leg for which regular massages and other treatments have been prescribed. Client says that she does not want to be a burden to her family taking her places and does not like handy ride services.

3. Consumer with serious and persistent mental illness (SPMI) says "Case workers don't understand what I need. When I ask for something, they say "you can do that for yourself". Well if I could do it myself, I would. What makes them think I like to ask for help? I am scared of taking the bus. I might get lost. Why is that taking advantage of the system?"

4. Student in elementary school referred to social worker for socialization group because he/she has gotten into fights with classmates." People bother you, you know? They want to get all into your business when it isn't none of their affair. Teachers never see what caused the fight; they just see the result of it. It is not fair, what is happening here. My old school was not like this."

5. Parent from Ghana in conflict with adolescent. "Parents in this country let their children do anything, say anything. In my country, it is a parent's job to keep their children out of trouble, make them see the difference between right and wrong. In this country, they say you are abusing your children."

Exercise 6.5
Role Plays Practicing Listening Skills

Goal: To employ all skills presented in the chapter in an appropriate way.

Focus Competencies or Practice Behaviors:
- EP 2.1.10a Substantively and affectively prepare for action with individuals, families, groups.
- EP 2.1.10b Use empathy and other interpersonal skills

This activity works best if there is an observer to the role play. Select one of the following situations or one of your choosing. Initiate a session and attempt to establish rapport. As appropriate, utilize paraphrases, reflections, summaries, seek concreteness, and focus. The observer for each situation can use the check list below to provide feedback. Carry out the role play for about 5 minutes then give feedback.

Consumer #1

Estrella was brought in by her mother, Maria, to you as a social worker at the battered women's shelter. Maria says that she was being battered by her husband. Estrella says that her mother pressured her into coming or she would never speak to her again.

Consumer # 2

Kay, 13, is on probation because she has attempted suicide and constantly talks about killing herself. You have been asked to be her clinical social worker. Her parents divorced, remarried with others, and now each has other children. She spends time with both families but is not strongly attached to either. She has assaulted her mother and half-sister. She often talks about violence, though these talks don't seem real but rather fantastic. She wants to get out of her mother's house and be free to spend time with peers. She sees no future and wonders if she will live beyond the summer.

Consumer #3

Tammy is a 16-year-old Native American adolescent. She has been admitted to a day treatment psychiatric hospital. She has spent some time in Portland with her dad. She attended modeling school and she loved it: she wants to be a runway model. She is on probation as a result of truancy, theft and chemical use (alcohol and marijuana). There are no other day treatment programs in the area so, while she had a theoretical choice, there wasn't another one in actuality. She denies involvement in theft and thinks that truancy and chemical use are nobody's business. She wants to get out of the "crazy hospital" as soon as soon as possible.

Consumer # 4

Your client is an international college student who has come to the Student Counseling Service because he (or she) is afraid about going crazy because he or she can't study, feels home sick and wonders whether leaving home to go to college was the right thing to do.

Name: _____ **Date:** _____

Supervisor's Name: _____

Focus Competencies:

- EP 2.1.4c Recognize and communicate their understanding of the importance of difference in shaping life experiences

- EP 2.1.4d View themselves as learners and engage those with whom they work as informants

- EP 2.1.10a Substantively and affectively prepare for action with individuals, families, groups, organizations, and communities

- EP 2.1.10b Use empathy and other interpersonal skills

Instructions: Evaluate your work or your partner's work in the Focus Practice Behaviors by completing the Practice Behaviors Assessment form below. What other Practice Behaviors did you use to complete these Exercises? Be sure to record them in your assessments. Please note that as you are beginning your work in this course, high level attainment of competencies at this point in your program is not anticipated. Over the course of this course and this program, your proficiency should increase to the point that you and other competent assessors will agree that you have attained the competency at a satisfactory level.

1.	I have attained this competency/practice behavior (in the range of 80 to 100%)
2.	I have largely attained this competency/practice behavior (in the range of 60 to 80%)
3.	I have partially attained this competency/practice behavior (in the range of 40 to 60%)
4.	I have made a little progress in attaining this competency/practice behavior (in the range of 20 to 40%
5.	I have made almost no progress in attaining this competency/practice behavior (in the range of 0 to 20%)

EPAS 2008 Core Competencies & Core Practice Behaviors	Student Self Assessment						Evaluator Feedback
Student and Evaluator Assessment Scale and Comments	0	1	2	3	4	5	Agree/Disagree/Comments
EP 2.1.1 Identify as a Professional Social Worker and Conduct Oneself Accordingly							
a. Advocate for client access to the services of social work							
b. Practice personal reflection and self-correction to assure continual professional development							

c. Attend to professional roles and boundaries								
d. Demonstrate professional demeanor in behavior, appearance, and communication								
e. Engage in career-long learning								
f. Use supervision and consultation								
EP 2.1.2 Apply Social Work Ethical Principles to Guide Professional Practice								
a. Recognize and manage personal values in a way that allows professional values to guide practice								
b. Make ethical decisions by applying NASW Code of Ethics and, as applicable, of the IFSW/IASSW Ethics in Social Work, Statement of Principles								
c. Tolerate ambiguity in resolving ethical conflicts								
d. Apply strategies of ethical reasoning to arrive at principled decisions								
EP 2.1.3 Apply Critical Thinking to Inform and Communicate Professional Judgments								
a. Distinguish, appraise, and integrate multiple sources of knowledge, including research-based knowledge and practice wisdom								
b. Analyze models of assessment, prevention, intervention, and evaluation								
c. Demonstrate effective oral and written communication in working with individuals, families, groups, organizations, communities, and colleagues								

EP 2.1.4 Engage Diversity and Difference in Practice							
a. Recognize the extent to which a culture's structures and values may oppress, marginalize, alienate, or create or enhance privilege and power							
b. Gain sufficient self-awareness to eliminate the influence of personal biases and values in working with diverse groups							
c. Recognize and communicate their understanding of the importance of difference in shaping life experiences							
d. View themselves as learners and engage those with whom they work as informants							
EP 2.1.5 Advance Human Rights and Social and Economic Justice							
a. Understand forms and mechanisms of oppression and discrimination							
b. Advocate for human rights and social and economic justice							
c. Engage in practices that advance social and economic justice							
EP 2.1.6 Engage in Research-Informed Practice and Practice-Informed Research							
a. Use practice experience to inform scientific inquiry							
b. Use research evidence to inform practice							
EP 2.1.7 Apply Knowledge of Human Behavior and the Social Environment							
a. Utilize conceptual frameworks to guide the processes of assessment, intervention, and evaluation							
b. Critique and apply knowledge to understand person and environment							
EP 2.1.8 Engage in Policy Practice to Advance Social and Economic Well-Being and to Deliver Effective Social Work Services							
a. Analyze, formulate, and advocate for policies that advance social well-being							

- 64 -

b. Collaborate with colleagues and clients for effective policy action							

<table>
<tr><td colspan="8">EP 2.1.9 Respond to Contexts that Shape Practice</td></tr>
</table>

a. Continuously discover, appraise, and attend to changing locales, populations, scientific and technological developments, and emerging societal trends to provide relevant services							
b. Provide leadership in promoting sustainable changes in service delivery and practice to improve the quality of social services							

<table>
<tr><td colspan="8">EP 2.1.10 Engage, Assess, Intervene, and Evaluate with Individuals, Families, Groups, Organizations and Communities</td></tr>
</table>

a. Substantively and affectively prepare for action with individuals, families, groups, organizations, and communities							
b. Use empathy and other interpersonal skills							
c. Develop a mutually agreed-on focus of work and desired outcomes							
d. Collect, organize, and interpret client data							
e. Assess client strengths and limitations							
f. Develop mutually agreed-on intervention goals and objectives							
g. Select appropriate intervention strategies							
h. Initiate actions to achieve organizational goals							
i. Implement prevention interventions that enhance client capacities							
j. Help clients resolve problems							
k. Negotiate, mediate, and advocate for clients							

l. Facilitate transitions and endings						
m. Critically analyze, monitor, and evaluate interventions						

Chapter 7
Eliminating Counterproductive Communication Patterns

Exercise 7.1
What Errors do you Observe?

Goal: to identify problems in professional demeanor and how to resolve them

Focus Competencies or Practice Behaviors:
- EP 2.1.1 Identify as a professional social worker and conduct one's self accordingly.
- EP 2.1.1b Practice personal reflection and self-correction to assure continual professional development
- EP 2.1.1d Demonstrate professional demeanor in behavior, appearance and communication

The video "Work with Probation Officer, Part 1" exemplifies a number of errors in conducting oneself as a professional social worker, practicing self-reflection and demonstrating professional demeanor.

1. Delineate specific examples of behavior, appearance and communication in part 1 that demonstrate a lack of professional behavior:

2. View "Work with a Probation Officer, Part 2" and compare the same aspects of behavior and assess whether they were performed with an appropriately professional demeanor:

3. View "Work with Corning Family, Session 1" and identify challenges to appropriate professional demeanor and speech:

4. View the final session of "Work with Corning Family" and assess the same behavior related to professional behavior and speech.

5. Have you observed interviews in person or conducted your own when inappropriate professional demeanor was demonstrated? Delineate what you saw.

6. Employing self-reflection, how might you or the person observed have modified this unprofessional behavior?

Exercise 7-2
What Am I Missing?

Goal: to become sensitive to possible sources of cross-cultural miscommunication.

Focus Competencies or Practice Behaviors:
- EP 2.1.4c Recognize and communicate their understanding of the importance of difference in shaping life experiences
- EP 2.1.4d View themselves as learners and engage those with whom they work as informants

Cultural differences may reflect differences of race or ethnicity or national origin. They may also reflect differences in sub-cultures of persons who may come from the same ethnic group. With each of the following videos, identify non-verbal behavioral patterns exhibited by the client(s). Explore possible interpretations for the meaning of that behavior. How might the social worker check out his or her perceptions?

1. The video "Getting back to Shakopee" features an interview between a Caucasian social worker and a Native American client.

   a. What behavioral and speech patterns do you notice from the client?

   b. How might you explain those patterns?

   c. How might you check out your understanding?

2. The video "Interview with Yan Ping" features an interview between a Caucasian social worker and a Chinese client.

   a. What behavioral and speech patterns do you notice from the client?

   b. How might you explain those patterns?

   c. How might you check out your understanding?

3. The video "Home for the Holidays, parts 1 & 2" features an interview between a Caucasian straight social worker and a lesbian couple.

   a. What behavioral and speech patterns do you notice from the clients?

   b. How might you explain those patterns?

   c. How might you check out your understanding?

4. The video "Work with Adolescent Parent and Foster Parent" features an interview between an African American social worker and two African American clients. The adolescent might, however, be considered as a member of a sub group of adolescent parents that are wards of the state that the social worker is not familiar with.

   a. What behavioral and speech patterns do you notice from the clients?

   b. How might you explain those patterns?

   c. How might you check out your understanding?

5. The video "Hanging with Hailey" features an interview between a Caucasian social worker and an Asian American adolescent client.

   a. What behavioral and speech patterns do you notice from the client?

   b. How might you explain those patterns How might these relate to her developmental stage?

   c. How might you check out your understanding?

6. The video " Serving the Squeaky Wheel" features an interview between a Caucasian social worker and a client who may be culturally similar to the social worker but who is diagnosed with a serious and persistent mental illness.

   a. What behavioral and speech patterns do you notice from the client?

b. How might you explain those patterns How might these relate to her developmental stage?

c. How might you check out your understanding?

7. Now reflect on any interview you have conducted or observed in which the client and social worker came from different groups.

a. What behavioral and speech patterns did you notice from the clients?

b. How might you explain those patterns?

c. How might you check out your understanding?

Exercise 7-3
Noticing Attending Behavior

Goal: To be able to notice when social worker are demonstrating attending behavior with.

Focus Competencies or Practice Behaviors:
- EP 2.1.10 Engage, assess, intervene and evaluate with individuals families and groups.
- EP 2.1.10b Use empathy and other interpersonal skills

Utilize the following table to assess physical attending behaviors. You may choose to assess one of the videos connected with the text or an interview you observe in person.

ASSESSING PHYSICAL ATTENDING BEHAVIORS	
Assessment	*Comments*
Direct eye contact Assess on a scale 0-4: 0 1 2 3 4	
Warmth and concern reflected in facial expression Assess on a scale 0-4: 0 1 2 3 4	

Eyes at same level as client's Assess on a scale 0-4: 0 1 2 3 4	
Appropriately varied and animated facial expressions Assess on a scale 0-4: 0 1 2 3 4	
Arms and hands moderately expressive; appropriate gestures Assess on a scale 0-4: 0 1 2 3 4	
Body leaning slightly forward; attentive but relaxed Assess on a scale 0-4: 0 1 2 3 4	
Voice clearly audible but not loud Assess on a scale 0-4: 0 1 2 3 4	
Warmth in tone of voice Assess on a scale 0-4: 0 1 2 3 4	
Voice modulated to reflect nuances of feeling and emotional tone of client messages Assess on a scale 0-4: 0 1 2 3 4	
Moderate speech tempo Assess on a scale 0-4: 0 1 2 3 4	
Absence of distracting behaviors (fidgeting, yawning, gazing out window, looking at watch)	

Assess on a scale 0-4: 0 1 2 3 4	
Other Assess on a scale 0-4: 0 1 2 3 4	

Exercise 7.4
Identifying Verbal Barriers to Communication

Goal: To be able to identify verbal barriers to communication that occur during interviews. .

Focus Competencies or Practice Behaviors:

- EP 2.1.1 Identify as a professional social worker and conduct ones self accordingly.
- EP 2.1.1b Practice personal reflection and self-correction to assure continual professional development
- EP 2.1.10a Substantively and affectively prepare for action with individuals, families, groups.
- EP 2.1.10b Use empathy and other interpersonal skills.

Utilize the table on the next page to assess verbal barriers to communication. You may choose to assess one of the videos connected with the text or an interview you observe in person.

ASSESSING VERBAL BARRIERS TO COMMUNICATION

Directions: In reviewing each 15-minute sample of taped interviews, tally your use of ineffective responses by placing marks in appropriate cells.

15-Minute Taped Samples	1	2	3	4
Reassuring, sympathizing, consoling, or excusing				
Advising and giving suggestions or solutions prematurely				
Using sarcasm or employing humour that is distracting or makes light of clients' problems				
Judging, criticizing, or placing blame				
Trying to convince the client about the right point of view through logical arguments, lecturing, instructing, or arguing				
Analyzing, diagnosing, or making glib or dogmatic interpretations				
Threatening, warning, or counterattacking				
Stacking questions				
Asking leading questions				
Interrupting inappropriately or excessively				
Dominating the interaction				

Fostering safe social interaction				
Responding infrequently				
Parroting or overusing certain phrases or clichés				
Dwelling on the remote past				
Going on fishing expeditions				
Other responses that impede communication. List:				

Exercise 7.5
Role Plays with Attending Behaviors and Avoiding Verbal Barriers to Communication

Goal: To carry out an interview demonstrating attending and avoiding verbal barriers to communication.

Focus Competencies or Practice Behaviors:

- EP 2.1.1 Identify as a professional social worker and conduct ones self accordingly.
- EP 2.1.1b Practice personal reflection and self-correction to assure continual professional development
- EP 2.1.10a Substantively and affectively prepare for action with individuals, families, groups.
- EP 2.1.10b Use empathy and other interpersonal skills.

This activity works best if there is an observer to the role play. Select one of the following situations or one of your choosing. The observer can monitor your employment of appropriate attending and avoidance of verbal barriers. The observer for each situation can use the tables above to provide feedback. Carry out the role play for about 5 minutes then give feedback.

Client #1

Adolescent female client in high school reports that she can't readily focus in class and was not turning in her homework on time. She reported that it was difficult to study at home and that she did not care for her mother's new boyfriend. Specifically, she did not like the fact that he is a smoker, that he seems lazy and has verbal fights with her mother. She tried to avoid him but that affects how she studies for school. She says she has a good relationship with her mother but is upset that her mother seems to care more about her boyfriend then she does about the client.

Client # 2

Young female single parent client has limited access to resources and social work intern has agreed to take her and her infant son shopping. She hands her son to intern. Her son is bundled up in winter clothes. She reports that she does not have a car seat for him and that she was going to just have him sit on her lap. She says that she needs groceries, pampers and other essentials badly.

Client # 3

Omar is 77 and attends an aging wellness center three times a week. He lives with his wife suffers from dementia and can not be left alone. Omar is generally upbeat and believes that persons should be stoic and put up with the adversities of life. The social work intern is aware of some respite services that Omar could qualify for..

Client # 4

Ms. Quinn has been referred to a children and family service by her son's school. She reports that she wants for her son Thomas' bad behavior to end. Specifically, she wants Thomas to say when he is mad or angry rather than hit, scream, or engage in other disruptive and dangerous behaviors when he is angry. Thomas is 8 and this behavior has accelerated since she was separated from her partner six months ago.

Chapter 7
Competencies/Practice Behaviors Exercises Assessment:

Name: _____ Date: _____

Supervisor's Name: _____

Focus Competencies:
- EP 2.1.1 Identify as a professional social worker and conduct one's self accordingly.
- EP 2.1.1b Practice personal reflection and self-correction to assure continual professional development
- EP 2.1.1d Demonstrate professional demeanor in behavior, appearance and communication
- EP 2.1.4c Recognize and communicate their understanding of the importance of difference in shaping life experiences
- EP 2.1.4.d View themselves as learners and engage those with whom they work as informants
- EP 2.1.10 Engage, assess, intervene and evaluate with individuals families and groups.
- EP 2.1.10a Substantively and affectively prepare for action with individuals, families, groups.
- EP 2.1.10b Use empathy and other interpersonal skills

Instructions: Evaluate your work or your partner's work in the Focus Practice Behaviors by completing the Practice Behaviors Assessment form below. What other Practice Behaviors did you use to complete these Exercises? Be sure to record them in your assessments. Please note that as you are beginning your work in this course, high level attainment of competencies at this point in your program is not anticipated. Over the course of this course and this program, your proficiency should increase to the point that you and other competent assessors will agree that you have attained the competency at a satisfactory level.

1.	I have attained this competency/practice behavior (in the range of 80 to 100%)
2.	I have largely attained this competency/practice behavior (in the range of 60 to 80%)
3.	I have partially attained this competency/practice behavior (in the range of 40 to 60%)
4.	I have made a little progress in attaining this competency/practice behavior (in the range of 20 to 40%
5.	I have made almost no progress in attaining this competency/practice behavior (in the range of 0 to 20%)

EPAS 2008 Core Competencies & Core Practice Behaviors	Student Self Assessment						Evaluator Feedback
Student and Evaluator Assessment Scale and Comments	0	1	2	3	4	5	Agree/Disagree/Comments
EP 2.1.1 Identify as a Professional Social Worker and Conduct Oneself Accordingly							
a. Advocate for client access to the services of social work							
b. Practice personal reflection and self-correction to assure continual professional development							
c. Attend to professional roles and boundaries							
d. Demonstrate professional demeanor in behavior, appearance, and communication							
e. Engage in career-long learning							
f. Use supervision and consultation							
EP 2.1.2 Apply Social Work Ethical Principles to Guide Professional Practice							
a. Recognize and manage personal values in a way that allows professional values to guide practice							
b. Make ethical decisions by applying NASW Code of Ethics and, as applicable, of the IFSW/IASSW Ethics in Social Work, Statement of Principles							
c. Tolerate ambiguity in resolving ethical conflicts							
d. Apply strategies of ethical reasoning to arrive at principled decisions							
EP 2.1.3 Apply Critical Thinking to Inform and Communicate Professional Judgments							
a. Distinguish, appraise, and integrate multiple sources of knowledge, including research-based knowledge and practice wisdom							
b. Analyze models of assessment, prevention, intervention, and evaluation							

- 77 -

c. Demonstrate effective oral and written communication in working with individuals, families, groups, organizations, communities, and colleagues							
EP 2.1.4 Engage Diversity and Difference in Practice							
a. Recognize the extent to which a culture's structures and values may oppress, marginalize, alienate, or create or enhance privilege and power							
b. Gain sufficient self-awareness to eliminate the influence of personal biases and values in working with diverse groups							
c. Recognize and communicate their understanding of the importance of difference in shaping life experiences							
d. View themselves as learners and engage those with whom they work as informants							
EP 2.1.5 Advance Human Rights and Social and Economic Justice							
a. Understand forms and mechanisms of oppression and discrimination							
b. Advocate for human rights and social and economic justice							
c. Engage in practices that advance social and economic justice							
EP 2.1.6 Engage in Research-Informed Practice and Practice-Informed Research							
a. Use practice experience to inform scientific inquiry							
b. Use research evidence to inform practice							
EP 2.1.7 Apply Knowledge of Human Behavior and the Social Environment							
a. Utilize conceptual frameworks to guide the processes of assessment, intervention, and evaluation							

b. Critique and apply knowledge to understand person and environment							

EP 2.1.8 Engage in Policy Practice to Advance Social and Economic Well-Being and to Deliver Effective Social Work Services							
a. Analyze, formulate, and advocate for policies that advance social well-being							
b. Collaborate with colleagues and clients for effective policy action							

EP 2.1.9 Respond to Contexts that Shape Practice							
a. Continuously discover, appraise, and attend to changing locales, populations, scientific and technological developments, and emerging societal trends to provide relevant services							
b. Provide leadership in promoting sustainable changes in service delivery and practice to improve the quality of social services							

EP 2.1.10 Engage, Assess, Intervene, and Evaluate with Individuals, Families, Groups, Organizations and Communities							
a. Substantively and affectively prepare for action with individuals, families, groups, organizations, and communities							
b. Use empathy and other interpersonal skills							
c. Develop a mutually agreed-on focus of work and desired outcomes							
d. Collect, organize, and interpret client data							
e. Assess client strengths and limitations							
f. Develop mutually agreed-on intervention goals and objectives							
g. Select appropriate intervention strategies							

h. Initiate actions to achieve organizational goals							
i. Implement prevention interventions that enhance client capacities							
j. Help clients resolve problems							
k. Negotiate, mediate, and advocate for clients							
l. Facilitate transitions and endings							
m. Critically analyze, monitor, and evaluate interventions							

Chapter 8
Assessment: Exploring and Understanding Problems and Strengths

Exercise 8.1
Applying the Cowger Matrix

Goal: To identify personal and environmental strengths and deficits, cased on a videotaped case.

Focus Competencies or Practice Behaviors:
1. EP 2.1.4c Recognize and communicate your understanding of the importance of difference in shaping life experiences
2. EP 2.1.7a Utilize conceptual frameworks to guide the processes of assessment, intervention, and evaluation
3. EP 2.1.7b Critique and apply knowledge to understand person and environment
4. EP 2.1.10a Substantively and affectively prepare for action with individuals, families, groups, organizations, and communities
5. EP 2.1.10d Collect, organize, and interpret client data
6. EP 2.1.10e Assess client strengths and limitations

Review the two videos associated with the text that feature Josephine, an older adult. Based on the case, identify the following (linked to Cowger's matrix).

1. Environmental factors that are strengths or resources

2. Personal factors that are strengths or resources

3. Environmental factors that are deficits, obstacles or challenges

4. Personal factors that are deficits, obstacles or challenges.

Goal: To understand the use of multiple data sources for social work assessment.

Focus Competencies or Practice Behaviors:

7. EP 2.1.3a Distinguish, appraise, and integrate multiple sources of knowledge, including research-based knowledge and practice wisdom
8. EP 2.1.4d View yourself as a learner and engage those with whom you work as informants
9. EP 2.1.7a Utilize conceptual frameworks to guide the processes of assessment, intervention, and evaluation
10. EP 2.1.7b Critique and apply knowledge to understand person and environment
11. EP 2.1.10a Substantively and affectively prepare for action with individuals, families, groups, organizations, and communities
12. EP 2.1.10d Collect, organize, and interpret client data
13. EP 2.1.10e Assess client strengths and limitations

For each of the following vignettes, list three different sources of data you would want to access in the case, beyond a client interview. Be specific! Don't just say "collateral contacts"; indicate who you would want to speak with and what you would want to learn. If you want to use observation, indicate the type and what you would be looking for.

1. A teenager referred to the school social worker because of troubling content in a creative writing assignment.

    -
    -
    -

2. A 30-year-old African American woman hospitalized with obesity, hypertension, and diabetes.

    -
    -
    -

3. A Latino family referred to a family service agency because they are concerned that their 13-year-old has "taken up with a bad crowd".

    -
    -
    -

4. An 80-year-old Caucasian female recently placed at assisted living who refuses to leave her room for meals and group activities.

    -
    -
    -

5. A middle-class family of four, referred to child protective services because the parents and the 9 year old twins share a bed at night and the youngsters are still being breast-fed.

    -
    -
    -

6. A 25 year old woman recently discharged from alcohol rehab who was referred to the community agency for urinalysis and aftercare services.

    -
    -
    -

Exercise 8.3
Theory-guided Assessment

Goal: To discover the measurements and resources available to guide assessments.

Focus Competencies or Practice Behaviors:
- EP 2.1.3a Distinguish, appraise, and integrate multiple sources of knowledge, including research-based knowledge and practice wisdom
- EP 2.1.3b Analyze models of assessment, prevention, intervention, and evaluation
- EP 2.1.7a Utilize conceptual frameworks to guide the processes of assessment, intervention, and evaluation
- EP 2.1.7b Critique and apply knowledge to understand person and environment
- EP 2.1.10a Substantively and affectively prepare for action with individuals, families, groups, organizations, and communities

Select a client from your caseload or one of the vignettes below. Using texts, journals and online resources, identify an assessment or treatment protocol manual, a measurement instrument, or other resource that would provide evidence-based guidance for assessment in the case. Then provide a link or citation for the resource and your analysis of the advantages and disadvantages of using the measurement or resource in assessment on the case.

Possible Cases

a. Cognitive-Behavioral approaches for military veterans with PTSD.

b. Solution-focused approaches for persons with eating disorders.

c. Task-centered approaches for improving parenting skills

d. Psychodynamic approaches for survivors of sexual trauma.

e. Assessment of suicide risk in elderly individuals.

f. Assessment of hoarding behavior.

g. Strengths-based assessment of children with autism-spectrum disorders.

Exercise 8.4
Strategies for Culturally Competent Assessment

Goal: To foster the skills to anticipate and identify differences in clients from various backgrounds.

Focus Competencies or Practice Behaviors:

- EP 2.1.3a Distinguish, appraise, and integrate multiple sources of knowledge, including research-based knowledge and practice wisdom

- EP 2.1.4b Gain sufficient self-awareness to eliminate the influence of personal biases and values in working with diverse groups

- EP 2.1.4c Recognize and communicate your understanding of the importance of difference in shaping life experiences

- EP 2.1.4d View yourself as a learner and engage those with whom you work as informants

- EP 2.1.7a Utilize conceptual frameworks to guide the processes of assessment, intervention, and evaluation

- EP 2.1.7b Critique and apply knowledge to understand person and environment

- EP 2.1.10a Substantively and affectively prepare for action with individuals, families, groups, organizations, and communities

- EP 2.1.10d Collect, organize, and interpret client data

- EP 2.1.10e Assess client strengths and limitations

Review content on culturally competent assessment in Chapter 8. For each client and presenting problem profiled, identify the considerations that you might anticipate if you were the social worker on the case. These issues might involve the client's goodness-of-fit with majority populations, the way that his or her difficulties are viewed within the cultural group and the larger society, cultural attitudes toward help seeking, the intersecting of multiple identities (gender/race and SES) and so on. Use online and written resources to identify recommendations the literature might have for understanding your client in the context of the contemporary United States and his or her presenting problem. In recognition of individual and within-group differences, identify at least two questions you would want to ask your client to better understand the impact of culture on his/her/their situation.

CASE 1: Latina mother and teenage daughter seeking help for the daughter's disobedience and truancy. They moved to the southeastern US when the daughter was 3.

- Anticipated Cultural Factors:

- Cultural Factors Suggested in the Literature:

- Questions for the Client about Culture:

CASE 2: A married African American male awaiting test results for HIV.

- Anticipated Cultural Factors:

- Cultural Factors Suggested in the Literature:

- Questions for the Client about Culture:

CASE 3: A 25-year-old Muslim man trying to find employment.

- Anticipated Cultural Factors:

- Cultural Factors Suggested in the Literature:

- Questions for the Client about Culture:

CASE 4: A 74-year-old woman from Somalia receiving in-home hospice care.

- Anticipated Cultural Factors:

- Cultural Factors Suggested in the Literature:

- Questions for the Client about Culture:

CASE 5: An Orthodox Jewish family whose son is being bullied and does not want to attend school.

- Anticipated Cultural Factors:

- Cultural Factors Suggested in the Literature:

- Questions for the Client about Culture:

CASE 6: A middle-aged Ethiopian doctor working as a hotel housekeeper in the US. She is experiencing Post Traumatic Stress Disorder following rape and other exposure to violence in her home country.

- Anticipated Cultural Factors:

- Cultural Factors Suggested in the Literature:

- Questions for the Client about Culture:

CASE 7: A lesbian seeking shelter for domestic violence.

- Anticipated Cultural Factors:

- Cultural Factors Suggested in the Literature:

- Questions for the Client about Culture:

CASE 8: A 12-year-old with disfiguring neurofibromatosis who has been referred to the school social worker for isolation and lack of friends.

- Anticipated Cultural Factors:

- Cultural Factors Suggested in the Literature:

- Questions for the Client about Culture:

Exercise 8.5
Critically Analyzing an Interview

Goal: To apply concepts on interviewing and problem exploration to a videotaped interview.

Focus Competencies or Practice Behaviors:
- EP 2.1.3a Distinguish, appraise, and integrate multiple sources of knowledge, including research-based knowledge and practice wisdom
- EP 2.1.3b Analyze models of assessment, prevention, intervention, and evaluation
- EP 2.1.7a Utilize conceptual frameworks to guide the processes of assessment, intervention, and evaluation
- EP 2.1.7b Critique and apply knowledge to understand person and environment
- EP 2.1.10a Substantively and affectively prepare for action with individuals, families, groups, organizations, and communities
- EP 2.1.10d Collect, organize, and interpret client data
- EP 2.1.10e Assess client strengths and limitations

Individually or in class, you should view the first "Yanping" video while completing this assignment. As you watch the video, identify whether the social worker, Kim, utilizes the assessment skills listed and whether she identified the major points of problem exploration. When you identify the items below, make note of the example you saw.

For any skills that were not demonstrated or areas that were not explored, provide an example of how the social worker could have addressed in with this client.

Alternatively, the instructor can divide the items among class participants so that each student is responsible for a limited number of items. Through whole-group discussion the class can compare and consolidate their findings.

Assessment Skills	Demonstrated (Y/N)	Example and/or Recommendation
The worker assesses problem of concern to client (including context, antecedents, conditions, emotional reactions)		
The worker assesses legal mandates (if applicable)		
The worker assesses for danger to self/others (if applicable)		
The worker uses appropriate open-ended questions (probing, exploration, clarification)		
The worker uses appropriate closed-ended questions		
The worker uses verbal following skills		
The worker paraphrases		
The worker employs empathic statements (level 3 or above)		

	Demonstrated (Y/N)	Example and/or Recommendation
The worker considers developmental stages appropriately		
The worker gathers information on strengths specifically		
The worker explores issues relayed to race, ethnicity/gender/sexual orientation, as applicable		
The worker explores spirituality		
The worker focuses the session on appropriate topics		
The worker summarizes periodically and at the end of the session		

Problem Exploration	Demonstrated (Y/N)	Example and/or Recommendation
The worker explores the client's concerns and problems as she and other concerned parties perceive them.		
The worker explores whether there are any current or impending legal mandates relevant to the situation.		
The worker explores whether any serious health or safety issues need immediate attention.		
The worker explores the specific indications of the problem, how it is manifesting itself, and the consequences.		

The worker explores who else is involved in the problem.		
The worker explores what unmet needs and/or wants are involved.		
The worker explores how developmental stages or life transitions affect the problem.		
The worker explores how ethnocultural, societal, and social class factors bear on the problem.		
The worker explores the severity of the problem and how it affects the client.		
The worker explores what meaning the client ascribes to the problem.		
The worker explores where, when, and how often problematic behaviors occur.		
The worker explores how long the problem gone on and why is the client seeking help now.		
The worker explores whether other issues (e.g., alcohol or substance abuse, physical or sexual abuse) are affecting the client's functioning.		

The worker explores the client's emotional reactions to the problem.		
The worker explores how the client has attempted to cope with the problem, and the required skills to resolve the problem.		
The worker explores the clients' skills, strengths, and resources.		
The worker explores what support systems exist or need to be created for the client.		
The worker explores what external resources the client needs?		

Role Play Exercise 8.6
The Collective Social Worker

Goal: To develop skills in collecting data and synthesizing findings into initial problem formulations.

Focus Competencies or Practice Behaviors:
- EP 2.1.4b Gain sufficient self-awareness to eliminate the influence of personal biases and values in working with diverse groups
- EP 2.1.4c Recognize and communicate your understanding of the importance of difference in shaping life experiences
- EP 2.1.4d View yourself as a learner and engage those with whom you work as informants
- EP 2.1.7a Utilize conceptual frameworks to guide the processes of assessment, intervention, and evaluation
- EP 2.1.7b Critique and apply knowledge to understand person and environment
- EP 2.1.10a Substantively and affectively prepare for action with individuals, families, groups, organizations, and communities
- EP 2.1.10d Collect, organize, and interpret client data
- EP 2.1.10e Assess client strengths and limitations

In this exercise the instructor will select a case from his or her practice experience or create a case from the following prompts. The instructor will portray the client in this interview.

- A new mother with symptoms of depression and loneliness.
- A recently widowed older adult.
- A teenager with symptoms of anxiety and perfectionism.
- An adult whose long-time partner/spouse has suddenly asked for a separation and moved out.
- A 19-year-old with a GED who cannot find work.

The class should be arranged in a horseshoe shape around the instructor. The instructor informs the class about the client's demographics, presenting problem and the setting for service. When the instructor sits, the role play commences, with the instructor playing the client in a first interview and the students portraying the collective social worker. (That is, the students share the responsibility of introducing the session and using interviewing skills to begin problem exploration. The pacing and sequencing of communications may be awkward because of the number of interviewers, but this should not affect the quality of the communication skills used or the findings.

After about 20 minutes (or when "the worker" seems at an impasse) the instructor should end the role play. Class members should then write assessments of the client based on the information gathered.

After class members have finished writing their assessments, the instructor should lead a discussion of the exercise. Suggested prompting questions include:

1. What interviewing and assessment skills did "the social worker" demonstrate?
2. How could the social worker have improved on the interview? What skills and elements of problem exploration were missing?
3. What did the worker learn about the client?
4. What information was not gathered that might be germane to the case?
5. Ask the students to exchange their assessments and compare their findings with those of their classmates. Were there differences in interpretations of the client's statements or demeanor? Discuss.

Name: _____ Date: _____

Supervisor's Name: _____

Focus Competencies/Practice Behaviors:

1. EP 2.1.3a Distinguish, appraise, and integrate multiple sources of knowledge, including research-based knowledge and practice wisdom
2. EP 2.1.3b Analyze models of assessment, prevention, intervention, and evaluation
3. EP 2.1.4b Gain sufficient self-awareness to eliminate the influence of personal biases and values in working with diverse groups
4. EP 2.1.4c Recognize and communicate your understanding of the importance of difference in shaping life experiences
5. EP 2.1.4d View yourself as a learner and engage those with whom you work as informants
6. EP 2.1.7a Utilize conceptual frameworks to guide the processes of assessment, intervention, and evaluation
7. EP 2.1.7b Critique and apply knowledge to understand person and environment
8. EP 2.1.10a Substantively and affectively prepare for action with individuals, families, groups, organizations, and communities
9. EP 2.1.10d Collect, organize, and interpret client data
10. EP 2.1.10e Assess client strengths and limitations

Instructions: Evaluate your work or your partner's work in the Focus Practice Behaviors by completing the Practice Behaviors Assessment form below. What other Practice Behaviors did you use to complete these Exercises? Be sure to record them in your assessments.

1.	I have attained this competency/practice behavior (in the range of 80 to 100%)
2.	I have largely attained this competency/practice behavior (in the range of 60 to 80%)
3.	I have partially attained this competency/practice behavior (in the range of 40 to 60%)
4.	I have made a little progress in attaining this competency/practice behavior (in the range of 20 to 40%
5.	I have made almost no progress in attaining this competency/practice behavior (in the range of 0 to 20%)

EPAS 2008 Core Competencies & Core Practice Behaviors	Student Self Assessment						Evaluator Feedback
Student and Evaluator Assessment Scale and Comments	0	1	2	3	4	5	Agree/Disagree/Comments
2.1.1 Identity as a Professional Social Worker and Conduct Oneself Accordingly:							
a. Advocate for client access to the services of social work							
b. Practice personal reflection and self-correction to assure continual professional development							

c. Attend to professional roles and boundaries							
d. Demonstrate professional demeanor in behavior, appearance, and communication							
e. Engage in career-long learning							
f. Use supervision and consultation							
2.1.2 Apply Social Work Ethical Principles to Guide Professional Practice:							
a. Recognize and manage personal values in a way that allows professional values to guide practice							
b. Make ethical decisions by applying NASW Code of Ethics and, as applicable, IFSW/IASSW Ethics in Social Work, Statement of Principles							
c. Tolerate ambiguity in resolving ethical conflicts							
d. Apply strategies in resolving ethical conflicts							
2.1.3 Apply Critical Thinking to Inform and Communicate Professional Judgments:							
a. Distinguish, appraise, and integrate multiple sources of knowledge, including research-based knowledge and practice wisdom							
b. Analyze models of assessment, prevention, intervention, and evaluation							
c. Demonstrate effective oral and written communication in working with individuals, families, groups, organizations, communities, and colleagues							
2.1.4 Engage Diversity and Difference in Practice:							
a. Recognize the extent to which a culture's structures and values may oppress, marginalize, alienate, or create or enhance privilege and power							
b. Gain sufficient self-awareness to eliminate the influence of personal biases and values in working with diverse groups							
c. Recognize and communicate their understanding of the importance of difference in shaping life experiences							

d. View themselves as learners and engage those with whom they work as informants							
2.1.5 Advance Human Rights and Social and Economic Justice							
a. Understand forms and mechanisms of oppression and discrimination							
b. Advocate for human rights and social and economic justice							
c. Engage in practices that advance social and economic justice							
2.1.6 Engage in research-informed practice and practice-informed research							
a. Use practice experience to inform scientific inquiry							
b. Use research evidence to inform practice							
2.1.7 Apply knowledge of human behavior and the social environment:							
a. Utilize conceptual frameworks to guide the processes of assessment, intervention, and evaluation							
b. Critique and apply knowledge to understand person and environment							
2.1.8 Engage in policy practice to advance social and economic well-being and to deliver effective social work services:							
a. Analyze, formulate, and advocate for policies that advance social well-being							
b. Collaborate with colleagues and clients for effective policy action							
2.1.9 Respond to contexts that shape practice:							
a. Continuously discover, appraise, and attend to changing locales, populations, scientific and technological developments, and emerging societal trends to provide relevant services							
b. Provide leadership in promoting sustainable changes in service delivery and practice to improve the quality of social services							
2.1.10 Engage, assess, intervene, and evaluate with individuals, families, groups, organizations and communities:							
a. Substantively and affectively prepare for action with individuals, families, groups, organizations, and communities							
b. Use empathy and other interpersonal skills							

c. Develop a mutually agreed-on focus of work and desired outcomes							
d. Collect, organize, and interpret client data							
e. Assess client strengths and limitations							
f. Develop mutually agreed-on intervention goals and objectives							
g. Select appropriate intervention strategies.							
h. Initiate actions to achieve organizational goals							
i. Implement prevention interventions that enhance client capacities							
j. Help clients resolve problems							
k. Negotiate, mediate, and advocate for clients							
l. Facilitate transitions and endings							
m. Critically analyze, monitor, and evaluate interventions							

Exercise 9.1
Applying an Ecosystems Perspective

Goal: To cultivate an ecosystems perspective by considering the systems and subsystems that may be involved in a given client situation.

Focus Competencies or Practice Behaviors:

- EP 2.1.3c Demonstrate effective oral and written communication in working with individuals, families, groups, organizations, communities, and colleagues
- EP 2.1.4c Recognize and communicate your understanding of the importance of difference in shaping life experiences
- EP 2.1.7a Utilize conceptual frameworks to guide the processes of assessment, intervention, and evaluation
- EP 2.1.7b Critique and apply knowledge to understand person and environment
- EP 2.1.10a Substantively and affectively prepare for action with individuals, families, groups, organizations, and communities
  EP 2.1.10d Collect, organize, and interpret client data
- EP 2.1.10e Assess client strengths and limitations

For each of the cases below, list the systems and subsystems that *might be* implicated in the problem or that may be part of its resolution. Recognize that these are hypotheses at this point in your work on the case. Client interviews and other data collection will help reveal the presence of these systems and the roles they play.

a. A couple that has just given birth to a child with Down's Syndrome

_____   _____
_____   _____
_____   _____
_____   _____
_____   _____

b. A 9-year-old who is grossly overweight.

_____   _____
_____   _____
_____   _____
_____   _____
_____   _____

c. A college student who was raped by an acquaintance.

_____   _____
_____   _____
_____   _____
_____   _____
_____   _____

d. A man whose wife of 60 years has died in a car accident in which he was driving.

_____   _____
_____   _____
_____   _____
_____   _____
_____   _____

e. A young adult whose family is concerned about his drug use.

_____   _____
_____   _____
_____   _____
_____   _____
_____   _____

Exercise 9.2
Assessment Vocabulary

Goal: Develop and demonstrate deep understanding of vocabulary and their use in practice.

Focus Competencies or Practice Behaviors:

- EP 2.1.3c Demonstrate effective oral and written communication in working with individuals, families, groups, organizations, communities, and colleagues
- EP 2.1.7a Utilize conceptual frameworks to guide the processes of assessment, intervention, and evaluation
- EP 2.1.7b Critique and apply knowledge to understand person and environment
- EP 2.1.10a Substantively and affectively prepare for action with individuals, families, groups, organizations, and communities

Using the letters on the list below, link the following terms with the portion of multidimensional assessment with which they are associated.

A.   Affective/emotional functioning

B.   Biophysical functioning

C.   Cognitive-perceptual functioning

D.   Behavioral functioning

E.   Environmental systems

____ Anhedonia	____ Labile	____ Coherence
____ Mania	____ Delusions	____ Appearance
____ Illnesses	____ Intelligence	____ Mood
____ Medications	____ Reality testing	____ Social support systems
____Substance use	____ Flight of ideas	____ Dementia
____ Judgment	____ Oriented X 3	____ Emotional constriction
____ Loose associations	____ Concentration	____ Safety
____ Dysphoria	____ Attire	____ Obsession
____ Values	____ Transportation	____ Perseveration
____ Executive functioning	____Misconceptions	____ Domineering
____ Aggression	____ Self-concept	____ Blunting
____ Physique	____ Disorganized	____ Bipolar disorder

Exercise 9.3
The Basics of a Mental Status Exam

Goal: To apply the concepts addressed in a mental status exam to a videotaped case.

Focus Competencies or Practice Behaviors:
- EP 2.1.3c Demonstrate effective oral and written communication in working with individuals, families, groups, organizations, communities, and colleagues
- EP 2.1.7a Utilize conceptual frameworks to guide the processes of assessment, intervention, and evaluation
- EP 2.1.10a Substantively and affectively prepare for action with individuals, families, groups, organizations, and communities
  EP 2.1.10d Collect, organize, and interpret client data
- EP 2.1.10e Assess client strengths and limitations

Review material in the text regarding the content of mental status exams (MSE), and review the video entitled "Serving the Squeaky Wheel." Complete the following elements of the MSE, using full sentences to depict the specific areas of the client's functioning. If there was no opportunity to observe certain features, indicate that in your evaluation.

At the completion of the exercise compare your findings with those of one or more classmates. In what ways do your assessments differ? What may have caused the differences? How can you incorporate the insights from this exercise to increase the accuracy, thoroughness, and objectivity of the MSEs you conduct?

1. Appearance

2. Reality Testing

3. Speech

4. Emotions

5. Thought content and processes

6. Sensory Perceptions

7. Mental Capacities

8. Attitude toward Interviewer

| **Exercise 9.5** |
| **Hard Question Skill Drill** |

Goal: To develop increased comfort with inquiry into difficult topics during assessment.

Focus Competencies or Practice Behaviors:
- EP 2.1.3c Demonstrate effective oral and written communication in working with individuals, families, groups, organizations, communities, and colleagues
- EP 2.1.10a Substantively and affectively prepare for action with individuals, families, groups, organizations, and communities

As you look back at Chapters 1 through 9, make note of the topics which made you feel uneasy. Of these, identify areas where you anticipate discomfort in conducting an assessment. This might include asking a client about past abuse, criminal history, income, sexual activity, substance use, aggression, suicidal intent, or other topics.

In the spaces below identify at least three questions that you feel would be difficult to discuss with a client. What is it that you fear in broaching the topic? Does it vary depending on the demographic background of the client or the nature of the setting?

Then below each question, identify at least 3 alternative ways of approaching the topic and asking what you need to know.

Next, work with a partner and allot at least 5 minutes for you to practice asking the questions. You can vary the ways you raise the topic, including your wording of the question and tone of voice. Your partner she should vary the response provided so that you get to experience a range of reactions (indignation, anger, hurt, compliance, etc). Try to keep responses brief so you can practice over and over. When the time is up, you and your partner should reverse roles and he or she should practice asking hard questions of you.

When the paired experience is complete, the instructor should lead a while group debriefing. The following are possible topics to address:

- What types of topics did the class find difficult?

- What themes were evident in the apprehensions class members had about certain topics.

- Did the skill drill help?

- What problems result when social workers avoid or skim over addressing difficult topics?

-What can social workers do to assure their competence in addressing difficult issues, and assure that they are responsive to their clients' needs over their own discomfort?

Difficult topic #1:

Nature of my discomfort:

Alternatives:

Difficult topic #2:

Nature of my discomfort:

Alternatives:

Difficult topic #3:

Nature of my discomfort:

Alternatives:

Role Play Exercise 9.6 **Suicide Lethality Assessment**

Goal: To increase familiarity and comfort with suicide lethality assessments though practice and discussion.

Focus Competencies or Practice Behaviors:

- EP 2.1.3c Demonstrate effective oral and written communication in working with individuals, families, groups, organizations, communities, and colleagues
- EP 2.1.4c Recognize and communicate your understanding of the importance of difference in shaping life experiences
- EP 2.1.7a Utilize conceptual frameworks to guide the processes of assessment, intervention, and evaluation
- EP 2.1.10a Substantively and affectively prepare for action with individuals, families, groups, organizations, and communities
  EP 2.1.10d Collect, organize, and interpret client data
- EP 2.1.10e Assess client strengths and limitations

For this exercise the instructor should construct role play opportunities in groups of three (client/social worker/observer) or group of the whole (everyone except client and social worker is an observer).

Students should review the material in Chapters 8 and 9 on suicide and lethality assessments. Next, develop a profile of a teenager who has been referred to the school social worker for unusual behavior in class (and who in fact is experiencing suicidal ideation). Create the case so that you can describe the client's background, social and family circumstances, suicide thoughts and plan, and the factors precipitating the suicidal ideation.

The focus of the role play is a first interview with the client which focuses on exploring the level of suicidal risk. The client should start the interview subtly indicating hopelessness or self-injury and then elaborate if the social worker explores suicide ideation. The role play need not proceed past the exploration of lethality.

When the role play is over, the instructor should debrief. The following questions can be used.

- What did the social worker feel he/she did well in the interview?

- What feedback can the client give the social worker about his or her work in the interview?

- How well did the social worker's interview align with the practice recommendations and risk factors in Chapters 8 and 9?

- What red flags were raised by the client's history and plan?

- If this were a real case, what could a social worker do to assist this client and assure his or her safety?

The discussion can be followed by other role plays for practice and insight through discussion.

Name: _____   **Date:** _____

Supervisor's Name: _____

Focus Competencies/Practice Behaviors:

- EP 2.1.3c Demonstrate effective oral and written communication in working with individuals, families, groups, organizations, communities, and colleagues

- EP 2.1.4c Recognize and communicate your understanding of the importance of difference in shaping life experiences

- EP 2.1.7a Utilize conceptual frameworks to guide the processes of assessment, intervention, and evaluation

- EP 2.1.7b Critique and apply knowledge to understand person and environment

- EP 2.1.10a Substantively and affectively prepare for action with individuals, families, groups, organizations, and communities
  EP 2.1.10d Collect, organize, and interpret client data

- EP 2.1.10e Assess client strengths and limitations

Instructions: Evaluate your work or your partner's work in the Focus Practice Behaviors by completing the Practice Behaviors Assessment form below. What other Practice Behaviors did you use to complete these Exercises? Be sure to record them in your assessments.

1.	I have attained this competency/practice behavior (in the range of 80 to 100%)
2.	I have largely attained this competency/practice behavior (in the range of 60 to 80%)
3.	I have partially attained this competency/practice behavior (in the range of 40 to 60%)
4.	I have made a little progress in attaining this competency/practice behavior (in the range of 20 to 40%
5.	I have made almost no progress in attaining this competency/practice behavior (in the range of 0 to 20%)

EPAS 2008 Core Competencies & Core Practice Behaviors	Student Self Assessment						Evaluator Feedback
Student and Evaluator Assessment Scale and Comments	0	1	2	3	4	5	Agree/Disagree/ Comments
2.1.1 Identity as a Professional Social Worker and Conduct Oneself Accordingly:							
a. Advocate for client access to the services of social work							
b. Practice personal reflection and self-correction to assure continual professional development							
c. Attend to professional roles and boundaries							

d. Demonstrate professional demeanor in behavior, appearance, and communication								
e. Engage in career-long learning								
f. Use supervision and consultation								
2.1.2 Apply Social Work Ethical Principles to Guide Professional Practice:								
a. Recognize and manage personal values in a way that allows professional values to guide practice								
b. Make ethical decisions by applying NASW Code of Ethics and, as applicable, IFSW/IASSW Ethics in Social Work, Statement of Principles								
c. Tolerate ambiguity in resolving ethical conflicts								
d. Apply strategies in resolving ethical conflicts								
2.1.3 Apply Critical Thinking to Inform and Communicate Professional Judgments:								
a. Distinguish, appraise, and integrate multiple sources of knowledge, including research-based knowledge and practice wisdom								
b. Analyze models of assessment, prevention, intervention, and evaluation								
c. Demonstrate effective oral and written communication in working with individuals, families, groups, organizations, communities, and colleagues								
2.1.4 Engage Diversity and Difference in Practice:								
a. Recognize the extent to which a culture's structures and values may oppress, marginalize, alienate, or create or enhance privilege and power								
b. Gain sufficient self-awareness to eliminate the influence of personal biases and values in working with diverse groups								
c. Recognize and communicate their understanding of the importance of difference in shaping life experiences								
d. View themselves as learners and engage those with whom they work as informants								
2.1.5 Advance Human Rights and Social and Economic Justice								
a. Understand forms and mechanisms of oppression and discrimination								
b. Advocate for human rights and social and economic justice								
c. Engage in practices that advance social and economic justice								

2.1.6 Engage in research-informed practice and practice-informed research							
a. Use practice experience to inform scientific inquiry							
b. Use research evidence to inform practice							
2.1.7 Apply knowledge of human behavior and the social environment:							
a. Utilize conceptual frameworks to guide the processes of assessment, intervention, and evaluation							
b. Critique and apply knowledge to understand person and environment							
2.1.8 Engage in policy practice to advance social and economic well-being and to deliver effective social work services:							
a. Analyze, formulate, and advocate for policies that advance social well-being							
b. Collaborate with colleagues and clients for effective policy action							
2.1.9 Respond to contexts that shape practice:							
a. Continuously discover, appraise, and attend to changing locales, populations, scientific and technological developments, and emerging societal trends to provide relevant services							
b. Provide leadership in promoting sustainable changes in service delivery and practice to improve the quality of social services							
2.1.10 Engage, assess, intervene, and evaluate with individuals, families, groups, organizations and communities:							
a. Substantively and affectively prepare for action with individuals, families, groups, organizations, and communities							
b. Use empathy and other interpersonal skills							
c. Develop a mutually agreed-on focus of work and desired outcomes							
d. Collect, organize, and interpret client data							
e. Assess client strengths and limitations							
f. Develop mutually agreed-on intervention goals and objectives							
g. Select appropriate intervention strategies.							
h. Initiate actions to achieve organizational goals							
i. Implement prevention interventions that enhance client capacities							
j. Help clients resolve problems							
k. Negotiate, mediate, and advocate for clients							
l. Facilitate transitions and endings							
m. Critically analyze, monitor, and evaluate interventions							

Exercise 10.1
Assessing the Jones Family

Goal: This exercise is designed to help you in assessing families using systems concepts.

Focus Competencies or Practice Behaviors:
- EP 2.1.1c Attend to professional roles and boundaries.
- EP 2.1.7a Utilize a conceptual framework to guide the process of assessment, intervention and evaluation.
- EP 2.1.7b Critique and apply knowledge to understand the person and environment.
- EP 2.1.10d Collect and organize client data

You are a social worker assigned to work with the Jones family. Read the case situation and answer the questions that follow.

The Jones family consists of both parents, and their four children. The family lives in a modest home in a changing urban neighborhood. Unlike some of their neighbors, however, Mr. and Mrs. Jones do not plan to move because they want to raise their children to be comfortable with differences. They are involved with a religious community and have a supportive network of extended family, friends and neighbors. Overall, the couple believed that their family was doing okay.

They have come to you seeking help because their household is filling with tension, which has caused their relationship to suffer. Trouble began for the family when Mr. Jones lost his full-time job at the automobile assembly plant. He has been fortunate to find work both as a handyman and as a snack and beverage vendor during professional sporting events. The work is seasonal, however, and the income is uncertain. The family manages to get by because Mrs. Jones is employed full-time as a home health aide. In addition, she works as a personal care attendant three evenings a week.

During a family meeting to discuss changes in family roles and responsibilities, Mr. Jones and the older child agreed that they assume responsibility for such household tasks as preparing the evening meals and lunches for the following day during the evening when Mrs. Jones was working.

As you listened to Mr. and Mrs. Jones in the initial session, they described conflict in their relationship as their primary concern. But each one emphasized a different reason as the source of their conflict. Mrs. Jones stated that she becomes angry because Mr. Jones sits on the couch watching television, drinking beer, and leaving the older child to do most of the tasks that he agreed to do, even on days when he is not working. Also, she stated that when she comes home from her evening job she has to finish cleaning the house and preparing the children's lunches for school the next day.

According to Mr. Jones, it is Mrs. Jones's expectations about the way that things should be done that has created tension and caused them to argue. For instance, in his opinion, leaving the evening meal's dishes in the sink for the next day was not a problem. To press his point, he asked for your opinion. Before you can respond, Mrs. Jones scoffs, and calls his behavior irresponsible. The constant stress of their financial situation seemed to be the one thing in which the couple is in agreement. Both are concerned about the future because they believe that their situation is unlikely to change any time soon given the state of the economy.

1. What is the interplay between the micro, mezzo, and macro factors in this case?

2. Discuss the interaction of the macro factors and their influence on the family and the relational dynamics between Mr. and Mrs. Jones.

3. Using the information that you provided in items A and B. write a brief assessment summary that highlights the Jones's family situation and that includes application of the systems concept of homeostasis.

Exercise 10.2
Responding to Mr. Jones

Goal: The goal is to assist you in understanding your professional role and boundaries

EP 2.1.1c Attend to professional role and boundaries

Recall that during the initial session with Mr. and Mrs. Jones, Mr. Jones asked for your opinion about the how he completed the household chores that he had agreed to do.

Invite a classmate to join you in a role-play, in which the classmate assumes the role of Mr. Jones.

1. During the role-play, what points did you emphasize in your response to Mr. Jones?

2. How did Mr. Jones react?

3. What skills would you use to maintain contact with Mr. Jones?

Exercise 10.3
Identifying and Utilizing Family Strengths

Goal: This exercise is designed to assist you in gathering information about family strengths.

Focus Competencies or Practice Behaviors:
- EP 2.1.10d Collect and organize client data
- EP 2.1.10e Assess client's strengths and limitations

Review the Jones's family case example and answer the following questions:

1. What are the strengths that you observed in the family as you read the case summary.

2. Develop a set of questions that you would ask to further explore strengths in this family.

3. Having observed and collected information on family strengths, describe how you would integrate this in your assessment of the family.

Exercise 10.4
What Would You Do?

Goal: To assist you in exploring family characteristics or family situations in which you might feel uncomfortable.

Focus Competencies or Practice Behaviors:
- 2.1.1b Practice self-reflection and self-correction to assure continual professional development.

- 2.1.2a Recognize and manage personal values in a way the allows professional values to guide practice
- 2.1.4c Recognize and communicate their understanding of the importance of differences in shaping life experiences.

To complete this exercise, partner with a classmate. Separately, the two of you should write a brief description of family characteristics or a family situation in which would feel uncomfortable.

After you and your classmate have completed the questions, discuss your answers.

1. Description of Family

2. Describe the specific concern or concerns that you might have.

3. What is the basis of your discomfort related to the concerns that you identified in the question above?

4. What do you know about the family that you described?

5. What steps would you take to learn more about the family?

6. In what way would learning more about the family ease your discomfort?

7. After answering all of the questions, write a summary about what you learned about yourself. In the summary, include aspects that you felt were strengths as well as areas for your future development.

8. Take turns discussing the result of this exercise with your peer partner.

Exercise 10.5
Who Should Decide?

Goal: The goal of this exercise is to help you in increasing your understanding of social workers' role when faced with diverse cultural values that influence family rules, roles, boundaries and decision-making.

Focus Competencies or Practice Behaviors:
- EP 2.1.1c Attend to professional roles and boundaries
- EP 2.1.4d Gain sufficient self-awareness to eliminate the influence of personal biases and values in working with diverse groups
- EP 2.1.2a Recognize personal values in a way that allows for professional values to guide practice
- EP 2.1.7b Critique and apply knowledge of the person and environment.

Read the following case situation which was presented by a team member who is a social worker during a recent team meeting.

The client is a 21-year-old university student, currently living in the home of her parents. The young woman was eight years of age when her parents immigrated to the United States. Even though they have accepted many US customs, they are reluctant to give up customs and beliefs from their country of origin. In fact, the parents believe that some of the US values are problematic for the family, and they have been selective in the values that they embrace.

In the initial session with the social worker, the client talked about her desire to move into her own apartment closer to the university campus. In her culture it is common for a single female to live in the home of her parents until she is married. So the question of her moving out and living alone is out of the question. When she talked to her parents about her desire to live alone, her father threatened to make her quit her studies at the university, believing that she had been unduly influenced by popular US culture.

The young woman works part-time on campus, so she would have the financial resources to rent an efficiency apartment. Her finances are, however, limited by other factors. For example, she tells you that one implicit family rule is that all family members contribute a portion of their earnings to help the rest part of the family living in their country of origin.

The social worker who presented the case believed that the family rules were rigid, and further that the attitude of the parents shortchanged the direction that the client wanted to take in her life. The social worker also asserted that she should have the right to pursue her own goals, which included managing the money that the client earned. In concluding the case presentation, the social worker indicated that she had encouraged the client to pursue a goal of achieving independence. She also asked the client's permission to meet with her parents so that she could educate them about the rights of young adults in the US.

1. What is your initial reaction to the situation?

2. What are the beliefs and values that guided the social worker's perspective in this case?

3. Discuss the clash between the specific values clash of the parents and the values of Western society and the values of the parents.

4. Describe the ways in which the parents manage the family's internal and external boundaries.

5. Describe the implicit rules and decision-making patterns in the family that govern family members' behavior.

6. As you listened to the team member's review of the case, what comments would you have wanted to make?

7. Other observations that you wish to make, based on your reading of the chapter.

Exercise 10.6
Considerations for Completing a Family Assessment

Goal: This exercise is designed to assist you in completing the various multiple tasks and integrating multiple sources of information needed in completing a family assessment.

Focus Competencies and Practice Behaviors

- EP 2.1.7a Utilize a conceptual framework to guide the processes of assessment, intervention, and evaluation
- EP 2.1.7b Critique and apply knowledge to understand the person and environment
- EP 2.1.10a Substantively and affectively prepare for action with individuals, families, groups communities and organizations
- EP 12.1.10b Use empathy and other interpersonal skills
- EP 2.1.10d Collect and organize client data

Using the prompts as guides, indicate how you would go about accomplishing the following.

1. Collaboration with the family

2. Using interpersonal and communications skills

3. Demonstrating Respect for Diversity

4. Applying system framework and concepts

5. Exploring resilience, strengths and risks

6. Understanding family stressors and transitions

7. Eliciting information about family relationship and communication patterns

8. Understanding the family's power structure

9. Gathering information about family goals

10. Assessing family decision-making

11. Analyzing the problem or concern presented by the family

12. Assessing your knowledge and skills in completing a family assessment

<table>
<tr><td colspan="2" align="center">**Chapter 10**
Competencies/Practice Behaviors Exercises Assessment:</td></tr>
</table>

Name: _____ **Date:** _____

Supervisor's Name: _____

Focus Competencies/Practice Behaviors:

- EP 2.1.1c Attend to professional roles and boundaries
- EP 2.1.4d Gain sufficient self-awareness to eliminate the influence of personal biases and values in working with diverse groups
- EP 2.1.2a Recognize personal values in a way that allows for professional values to guide practice
- EP 2.1.7a Utilize a conceptual framework to guide the process of assessment, intervention and evaluation.
- EP 2.1.7b Critique and apply knowledge to understand the person and environment.
- EP 2.1.10b Use empathy and other interpersonal skills
- EP 2.1.10d Collect and organize client data
- EP 2.1.10e Assess client's strengths and limitations

Instructions: Evaluate your work or your partner's work in the Focus Practice Behaviors by completing the Practice Behaviors Assessment form below. What other Practice Behaviors did you use to complete these Exercises? Be sure to record them in your assessments.

1.	I have attained this competency/practice behavior (in the range of 80 to 100%)
2.	I have largely attained this competency/practice behavior (in the range of 60 to 80%)
3.	I have partially attained this competency/practice behavior (in the range of 40 to 60%)
4.	I have made a little progress in attaining this competency/practice behavior (in the range of 20 to 40%
5.	I have made almost no progress in attaining this competency/practice behavior (in the range of 0 to 20%)

EPAS 2008 Core Competencies & Core Practice Behaviors	Student Self Assessment						Evaluator Feedback
Student and Evaluator Assessment Scale and Comments	0	1	2	3	4	5	Agree/Disagree/Comments
2.1.1 Identity as a Professional Social Worker and Conduct Oneself Accordingly:							
a. Advocate for client access to the services of social work							
b. Practice personal reflection and self-correction to assure continual professional development							
c. Attend to professional roles and boundaries							

d. Demonstrate professional demeanor in behavior, appearance, and communication							
e. Engage in career-long learning							
f. Use supervision and consultation							
2.1.2 Apply Social Work Ethical Principles to Guide Professional Practice:							
a. Recognize and manage personal values in a way that allows professional values to guide practice							
b. Make ethical decisions by applying NASW Code of Ethics and, as applicable, IFSW/IASSW Ethics in Social Work, Statement of Principles							
c. Tolerate ambiguity in resolving ethical conflicts							
d. Apply strategies in resolving ethical conflicts							
2.1.3 Apply Critical Thinking to Inform and Communicate Professional Judgments:							
a. Distinguish, appraise, and integrate multiple sources of knowledge, including research-based knowledge and practice wisdom							
b. Analyze models of assessment, prevention, intervention, and evaluation							
c. Demonstrate effective oral and written communication in working with individuals, families, groups, organizations, communities, and colleagues							
2.1.4 Engage Diversity and Difference in Practice:							
a. Recognize the extent to which a culture's structures and values may oppress, marginalize, alienate, or create or enhance privilege and power							
b. Gain sufficient self-awareness to eliminate the influence of personal biases and values in working with diverse groups							
c. Recognize and communicate their understanding of the importance of difference in shaping life experiences							

d. View themselves as learners and engage those with whom they work as informants							
2.1.5 Advance Human Rights and Social and Economic Justice							
a. Understand forms and mechanisms of oppression and discrimination							
b. Advocate for human rights and social and economic justice							
c. Engage in practices that advance social and economic justice							
2.1.6 Engage in research-informed practice and practice-informed research							
a. Use practice experience to inform scientific inquiry							
b. Use research evidence to inform practice							
2.1.7 Apply knowledge of human behavior and the social environment:							
a. Utilize conceptual frameworks to guide the processes of assessment, intervention, and evaluation							
b. Critique and apply knowledge to understand person and environment							
2.1.8 Engage in policy practice to advance social and economic well-being and to deliver effective social work services:							
a. Analyze, formulate, and advocate for policies that advance social well-being							
b. Collaborate with colleagues and clients for effective policy action							
2.1.9 Respond to contexts that shape practice:							
a. Continuously discover, appraise, and attend to changing locales, populations, scientific and technological developments, and emerging societal trends to provide relevant services							
b. Provide leadership in promoting sustainable changes in service delivery and practice to improve the quality of social services							
2.1.10 Engage, assess, intervene, and evaluate with individuals, families, groups, organizations and communities:							
a. Substantively and affectively prepare for action with individuals, families, groups, organizations, and communities							

- 117 -

b. Use empathy and other interpersonal skills							
c. Develop a mutually agreed-on focus of work and desired outcomes							
d. Collect, organize, and interpret client data							
e. Assess client strengths and limitations							
f. Develop mutually agreed-on intervention goals and objectives							
g. Select appropriate intervention strategies.							
h. Initiate actions to achieve organizational goals							
i. Implement prevention interventions that enhance client capacities							
j. Help clients resolve problems							
k. Negotiate, mediate, and advocate for clients							
l. Facilitate transitions and endings							
m. Critically analyze, monitor, and evaluate interventions							

Chapter 11
Forming and Assessing Social Work Groups

Exercise 11.1
Identifying with Group Concepts

Goal: To increase understanding of group concepts by applying them to past or current group experiences.

Focus Competencies or Practice Behaviors:

- EP2.1.7a Utilize conceptual frameworks to guide the processes of assessment, intervention, and evaluation
- EP2.1.10a Substantively and affectively prepare for action with individuals, families, groups, organizations, and communities

List at least 5 groups that you can recall participating in since your teenage years. These may include classes, clubs, group assignments, sorority or fraternity, teams, committees, support or therapy groups or groups organized around hobbies, interests, politics or faith communities.

Place an asterisk (*) by those groups you felt were particularly effective and a hash mark (#) by those you felt were not. Now, choose one effective group and one ineffective group to address the following questions:

Effective Group:

1. What was the group purpose?

2. What was the type of group?

3. Was it open or closed membership?

4. Was it open or closed in length?

5. Was your membership voluntary or involuntary?

6. How often did it meet?

7. How long was each meeting?

8. Describe the composition (number of members, areas of homogeneity or diversity):

9. Describe some rules or norms that emerged in the group:

10. Describe the leadership. How did that contribute to group success?

11. What were the signs that the group was effective? Do you think any members found it unhelpful or unsuccessful?

12. Consider the factors above and other advice about successful groups contained in Chapter 11 and describe the reasons you believe that this particular group experience was successful.

Ineffective Group:

1. What was the group purpose?

2. What was the type of group?

3. Was it open or closed membership?

4. Was it open or closed in length?

5. Was your membership voluntary or involuntary?

6. How often did it meet?

7. How long was each meeting?

8. Describe the composition (number of members, areas of homogeneity or diversity):

9. Describe some rules or norms that emerged in the group:

10. Describe the leadership. How did that contribute to group success?

11. What were the signs that the group was effective? Do you think any members found it unhelpful or unsuccessful?

12. Consider the factors above and other advice about successful groups contained in Chapter 11 and describe the reasons you believe that this particular group experience was successful.

Exercise 11.2
Planning New Groups

Goal: To apply the concepts of planning to hypothetical social work groups.

Focus Competencies or Practice Behaviors:
- EP2.1.4c Recognize and communicate understanding of the importance of difference in shaping life experiences
- EP2.1.7a Utilize conceptual frameworks to guide the processes of assessment, intervention, and evaluation
- EP2.1.10a Substantively and affectively prepare for action with individuals, families, groups, organizations, and communities

Separate into groups of 5 and assign individuals to the topics associated with their respective number (1s do 1, 2s do 2, etc.):

Topic 1: A support group for people whose spouses have deployed in the military.

Topic 2: An advocacy group for parents whose children are enrolled in special education

Topic 3: An inpatient group for children with cancer.

Topic 4: A life-skills group for teens who are aging out of foster care

Topic 5: A support group for siblings of children with Downs Syndrome.

Using the guidelines in Chapter 11, each student should design a group, determining:
1. The name he/she will give the group
2. The type of group
3. A one-sentence statement of purpose
4. The size of the group
5. The length of the group
6. The location where it will meet
7. Important factors in group composition
8. How he/she will recruit and screen members

Next, all members assigned to the same topic should compare the plans they devised. The groups should discuss each member's rationale for his/her choices about their plans and the pros and cons of the various plans.

Finally, each group should share one of their plans verbally with the rest of the class.

Exercise 11.3
Designing Group Programming

Goal: To develop skills and knowledge in group planning.

Focus Competencies or Practice Behaviors:
- EP 2.1.2b Make ethical decisions by applying standards of the National Association of Social Workers Code of Ethics and, as applicable, of the International Federation of Social Workers/International Association of Schools of Social Work Ethics in Social Work, Statement of Principles
- EP2.1.6b Use research evidence to inform practice
- EP2.1.7a Utilize conceptual frameworks to guide the processes of assessment, intervention, and evaluation
- EP2.1.10a Substantively and affectively prepare for action with individuals, families, groups, organizations, and communities
- EP 2.1.10.j Help clients resolve problems

Select one of the following group topics.

   Topic 1: A group for people whose spouses have deployed in the military.

   Topic 2: A group for people who hoard food and objects.

   Topic 3: A group for teens who are aging out of foster care.

   Topic 4: A group for family members caring for persons with Alzheimer's disease.

   Topic 5: A group for siblings of children with disabilities.

Design the curriculum for a 10 week educational and support group on the topic. Use the spaces below list the activities, presentations and/or discussion topics you would utilize each week. Each group meeting is 90 minutes long and you are free to research best practices available and consider adopting them for your group plan. After you have created your curriculum, answer the discussion questions.

Your instructor may organize the class into sub-groups or facilitate discussion in the whole group about the insights and plans generated by this exercise.

Week One

Week Two

Week Three

Week Four

Week Five

Week Six

Week Seven

Week Eight

Week Nine

Week Ten

Discussion Question 1: What features of the topic, client population, timing, etc. did you take into account in planning the sessions?

Discussion Question 2: How did you decide what to include in the sessions? If you referred to outside resources, were they helpful?

Discussion Question 3: Which elements of this assignment came most easily to you and which did you find difficult?

Discussion Question 4: Does the plan require special expertise or preparation by the social worker?

Discussion Question 5: Is the plan suitable for clients from a variety of racial, ethnic, SES and other backgrounds?

Exercise 11.4
Ethics in Group Work

Goal: To practice ethical decision making on the dilemmas that can arise in group work.

Focus Competencies or Practice Behaviors:
- EP 2.1.2b Make ethical decisions by applying standards of the National Association of Social Workers Code of Ethics and, as applicable, of the International Federation of Social Workers/International Association of Schools of Social Work Ethics in Social Work, Statement of Principles
- EP2.1.2c Tolerate ambiguity in resolving ethical conflicts
- EP2.1.2d Apply strategies of ethical reasoning to arrive at principled decisions
- EP2.1.4c Recognize and communicate understanding of the importance of difference in shaping life experiences
- EP2.1.7a Utilize conceptual frameworks to guide the processes of assessment, intervention, and evaluation
- EP2.1.10a Substantively and affectively prepare for action with individuals, families, groups, organizations, and communities

Using one or more of the following cases, engage in group discussion of the dilemma presented, using the following steps adapted from Chapter 4. Alternatively, the instructor may break the class into small groups and assign each group to answer one of the steps then bring them together to compile the results, weigh the options, and arrive at a decision. The class should then engage in a whole-group discussion of the strategies to effectively *carry out* the decision and the ways that the effectiveness of the decision could be evaluated.

1. What is the problem or dilemma? (Gather as much information about the situation from as many perspectives as possible, including that of the client).
2. What core principles and the competing issues are imbedded in the case?
3. What do Codes of Ethics suggest for responding to the case?
4. What laws, policies, and regulations apply to the case?
5. Who should the social worker(s) consult with in resolving the dilemma?
6. What are the possible and probable courses of action? What are the consequences of various options?

Case One: The social worker facilitates a youth group at her church/temple/mosque as part of an after school enrichment program. One of the youngsters has autism and his behaviors are sometimes disruptive to the group and upsetting to the members. Because of this, some members have quit the group or been removed by their parents. The group is still needed, but soon will scarcely have any members left.

Case Two: In a community based group of adults with severe and persistent mental illness, one of the members tells the others he is getting married and produces a picture of his fiancé that is obviously one that came with the frame. The other group members do not seem skeptical of the man's claims and initiate an extended discussion of how they can support him as his life changes after his marriage. They also take up a collection to buy the man and his bride a gift. The worker is certain the member is lying and cannot now extricate himself from his story.

Case Three: In a support group at a domestic violence agency, one of the women reveals that her boyfriend also hit her children when they tried to intercede in her abuse. She states, "I'm glad were all safe here now so child welfare doesn't get all over me about it".

Case Four: In the first session of a bereavement group, the social worker realizes that one of the members is her hairdresser/his barber.

Case Five: In a group for former inmates who have returned to the community, the members express remorse for crimes they have committed and the desire to leave that life behind. They also share information about crimes currently being committed in the community by their gangs including car jacking and sexual trafficking.

Exercise 11.5
Manualized Groups

Goal: To be able to critically examine empirically-supported models of group treatment.

Focus Competencies or Practice Behaviors:
- EP 2.1.2b Make ethical decisions by applying standards of the National Association of Social Workers Code of Ethics and, as applicable, of the International Federation of Social Workers/International Association of Schools of Social Work Ethics in Social Work, Statement of Principles
- EP2.1.3b Analyze models of assessment, prevention, intervention, and evaluation
- EP2.1.4c Recognize and communicate understanding of the importance of difference in shaping life experiences
- EP2.1.6b Use research evidence to inform practice
- EP2.1.7a Utilize conceptual frameworks to guide the processes of assessment, intervention, and evaluation
- EP2.1.10a Substantively and affectively prepare for action with individuals, families, groups, organizations, and communities

Select one of the following problem areas:
- Depression
- Obesity
- Somataform pain disorders
- Anxiety
- Conduct disorder
- Anger management
- Social phobia
- Substance abuse
- Post-traumatic stress disorder

Using online searches find information on a manualized protocol for group therapy to address the problem. Then answer the following questions:

1. What advice does the online resource provide about how to structure the group?

   a. Characteristics of members?

   b. Size of group?

   c. Number of sessions?

d. Content of sessions?

e. Appropriateness for diverse population groups?

2. Could you have downloaded enough information to adopt it for use as a group leader? If not, what fees, knowledge or resources would be needed for you to learn how to do the group according to the manual?

3. What procedures are used for evaluating success in the group?

4. What procedures are recommended so that leaders adopt and use the group guidelines in a uniform fashion (with fidelity)?

5. How persuasive is the evidence that this group model is effective?

Role Play Exercise 11.6
Skills in the Pre-Affiliation Phase

Goal: To practice screening and selection of potential group members

Focus Competencies or Practice Behaviors:
- EP 2.1.2b Make ethical decisions by applying standards of the National Association of Social Workers Code of Ethics and, as applicable, of the International Federation of Social Workers/International Association of Schools of Social Work Ethics in Social Work, Statement of Principles
- EP2.1.4c Recognize and communicate understanding of the importance of difference in shaping life experiences
- EP2.1.7a Utilize conceptual frameworks to guide the processes of assessment, intervention, and evaluation

- EP2.1.10a Substantively and affectively prepare for action with individuals, families, groups, organizations, and communities
- EP2.1.10d Collect, organize, and interpret client data
- EP2.1.10e Assess client strengths and limitations
- EP 2.1.10.j Help clients resolve problems

Your instructor should divide the class into 4 groups. Each group should be assigned one of the following group topics.

Topic A: Involuntary anger management group for court-referred adults.

Topic B: A group for people who hoard food and objects.

Topic C: A group for family members of murder victims.

Topic D: A group for teenage girls who have overweight.

First, review the guidelines for conducting preliminary interviews, found in Chapter 11 and discuss the kinds of questions that should be addressed in a pre-screening interview for prospective group members. Next, pair with a partner from one of the other groups and take turns role playing the social worker and the prospective client. Role play the preliminary interviews, switching roles (and settings) when the first is complete.

After the role-play are complete, discussion the experiences, observations, and suggestions that resulted from the role play as a class. Specifically: Did the interview provide sufficient information for the worker to decide that the client was appropriate for the group and for the client to decide if the group was appropriate for him/her? Did the role play meet the objectives of preliminary interviews (information sharing, relationship building, identifying experiences, apprehensions and needs for the prospective group member? etc.) Was the interviewer culturally competent and sensitive to other aspects the client presented?

Chapter 11
Competencies/Practice Behaviors Exercises Assessment:

Name: _____ **Date:** _____

Supervisor's Name: _____

Focus Competencies/Practice Behaviors:

- EP 2.1.2b Make ethical decisions by applying standards of the National Association of Social Workers Code of Ethics and, as applicable, of the International Federation of Social Workers/International Association of Schools of Social Work Ethics in Social Work, Statement of Principles
- EP2.1.2c Tolerate ambiguity in resolving ethical conflicts
- EP2.1.2d Apply strategies of ethical reasoning to arrive at principled decisions
- EP2.1.3b Analyze models of assessment, prevention, intervention, and evaluation
- EP2.1.4c Recognize and communicate understanding of the importance of difference in shaping life experiences
- EP2.1.6b Use research evidence to inform practice
- EP2.1.7a Utilize conceptual frameworks to guide the processes of assessment, intervention, and evaluation
- EP2.1.10a Substantively and affectively prepare for action with individuals, families, groups, organizations, and communities
- EP2.1.10d Collect, organize, and interpret client data
- EP2.1.10e Assess client strengths and limitations
- EP 2.1.10.j Help clients resolve problems

Instructions: Evaluate your work or your partner's work in the Focus Practice Behaviors by completing the Practice Behaviors Assessment form below. What other Practice Behaviors did you use to complete these Exercises? Be sure to record them in your assessments.

1.	I have attained this competency/practice behavior (in the range of 80 to 100%)
2.	I have largely attained this competency/practice behavior (in the range of 60 to 80%)
3.	I have partially attained this competency/practice behavior (in the range of 40 to 60%)
4.	I have made a little progress in attaining this competency/practice behavior (in the range of 20 to 40%
5.	I have made almost no progress in attaining this competency/practice behavior (in the range of 0 to 20%)

EPAS 2008 Core Competencies & Core Practice Behaviors	Student Self Assessment						Evaluator Feedback
Student and Evaluator Assessment Scale and Comments	0	1	2	3	4	5	Agree/Disagree/Comments
2.1.1 Identity as a Professional Social Worker and Conduct Oneself Accordingly:							
a. Advocate for client access to the services of social work							
b. Practice personal reflection and self-correction to assure continual professional development							

c. Attend to professional roles and boundaries							
d. Demonstrate professional demeanor in behavior, appearance, and communication							
e. Engage in career-long learning							
f. Use supervision and consultation							
2.1.2 Apply Social Work Ethical Principles to Guide Professional Practice:							
a. Recognize and manage personal values in a way that allows professional values to guide practice							
b. Make ethical decisions by applying NASW Code of Ethics and, as applicable, IFSW/IASSW Ethics in Social Work, Statement of Principles							
c. Tolerate ambiguity in resolving ethical conflicts							
d. Apply strategies in resolving ethical conflicts							
2.1.3 Apply Critical Thinking to Inform and Communicate Professional Judgments:							
a. Distinguish, appraise, and integrate multiple sources of knowledge, including research-based knowledge and practice wisdom							
b. Analyze models of assessment, prevention, intervention, and evaluation							
c. Demonstrate effective oral and written communication in working with individuals, families, groups, organizations, communities, and colleagues							
2.1.4 Engage Diversity and Difference in Practice:							
a. Recognize the extent to which a culture's structures and values may oppress, marginalize, alienate, or create or enhance privilege and power							
b. Gain sufficient self-awareness to eliminate the influence of personal biases and values in working with diverse groups							
c. Recognize and communicate their understanding of the importance of difference in shaping life experiences							

d. View themselves as learners and engage those with whom they work as informants	

2.1.5 Advance Human Rights and Social and Economic Justice

a. Understand forms and mechanisms of oppression and discrimination	
b. Advocate for human rights and social and economic justice	
c. Engage in practices that advance social and economic justice	

2.1.6 Engage in research-informed practice and practice-informed research

a. Use practice experience to inform scientific inquiry	
b. Use research evidence to inform practice	

2.1.7 Apply knowledge of human behavior and the social environment:

a. Utilize conceptual frameworks to guide the processes of assessment, intervention, and evaluation	
b. Critique and apply knowledge to understand person and environment	

2.1.8 Engage in policy practice to advance social and economic well-being and to deliver effective social work services:

a. Analyze, formulate, and advocate for policies that advance social well-being	
b. Collaborate with colleagues and clients for effective policy action	

2.1.9 Respond to contexts that shape practice:

a. Continuously discover, appraise, and attend to changing locales, populations, scientific and technological developments, and emerging societal trends to provide relevant services	
b. Provide leadership in promoting sustainable changes in service delivery and practice to improve the quality of social services	

2.1.10 Engage, assess, intervene, and evaluate with individuals, families, groups, organizations and communities:

a. Substantively and affectively prepare for action with individuals, families, groups, organizations, and communities	

- 131 -

b. Use empathy and other interpersonal skills							
c. Develop a mutually agreed-on focus of work and desired outcomes							
d. Collect, organize, and interpret client data							
e. Assess client strengths and limitations							
f. Develop mutually agreed-on intervention goals and objectives							
g. Select appropriate intervention strategies.							
h. Initiate actions to achieve organizational goals							
i. Implement prevention interventions that enhance client capacities							
j. Help clients resolve problems							
k. Negotiate, mediate, and advocate for clients							
l. Facilitate transitions and endings							
m. Critically analyze, monitor, and evaluate interventions							

Exercise 12.1
Getting From Point A to Point B

Goal: To assist you in developing and writing goals.

Focus on Practice Behaviors:
- EP 2.1.10c Develop a mutually agreed-on focus of work and desired outcomes.
- EP 2.1.10j Help clients solve problems

Read the case example, and using the prompts as guides answer the questions and complete the tasks that follow.

Agnes, age 6, Cody, age 8, and Jennifer, age 10, were removed from the custody of their parents because of hazardous, unsanitary conditions in the home environment and nutritional neglect. The judge's order stated that the children would be returned home if there was sufficient evidence that hazards in the home had been removed and that the children had nutritious meals. When you met the parents they were angry about the court's mandate, but the agreed to comply with the judge's order because they wanted the children to be returned home. Even so, they demanded that you explain to them what the judge meant by hazardous, unsanitary conditions and nutritional neglect.

During the meeting, you work with the parents to develop a goal so that they can regain custody of their children.

1. Write explicit definition of the two target problems in this case.

   a. Hazardous, unsanitary conditions:

   b. Nutritional neglect:

2. Select one of the above as the priority target problem and develop a goal.

3. Identify the goal as covert or overt, or a combination of both.

4. Identify potential barriers to goal attainment.

5. Using the rating scale below, 1 (low) and 5 (high) evaluate the goal that you developed with the parents based on the following criteria.

Criteria	Rating				
Goals is linked to the target problem	1	2	3	4	5
Goal is specific	1	2	3	4	5
Goal is defined in explicit and measurable terms	1	2	3	4	5
Goal is feasible	1	2	3	4	5
Desired level of change	1	2	3	4	5
Goal language is positive and emphasizes growth	1	2	3	4	5

6. How well your goal met the above criteria?

7. Based on your self-evaluation, indicate where improvement is indicated and write a goal for yourself.

Exercise 12.2
Reaching the Final Destination Point

Goal: To assist you in applying your skills in the process of developing tasks and measuring progress.

Focus Competencies and Practice Behaviors
- EP 2.1.10j Helping clients solve problems
- EP 2.1.10m Critically analyze, monitor and evaluate interventions

Continuing your work with parents in the above case example, develop general and specific tasks that the parents will complete to accomplish their goal.

Describe how you would monitor and measure progress in the case.

1. Restate the Priority Goal:

2. General Task:

3. Specific tasks (action steps):

4. Describe the methods to be used to monitor and measure progress using a qualitative and a quantitative method:

5. Using Figure 12-3 in the text, write 3-4 case progress notes entries

| **Exercise 12.3** |
| **Don't Tell Me What To Do!** |

Goal: To apply strategies in developing goals with involuntary clients

Focus Competencies and Practice Behaviors
- EP 2.1.1.1f Use Supervision and Consultation
- EP 2.1.10c Develop a mutually agreed-on focus of work and desired outcomes
- EP 2.1.10i Implement prevention interventions that enhance client capacities
- EP 2.1.10j Helping clients solve problems

Following the prompts write a brief summary of the strategies that are intended to facilitate developing goals with involuntary clients.

- Motivational Congruence:

- Agreeable Mandate:

- Let's Make a Deal:

- Getting Rid of the Mandate:

Now, read the case example and indicate which of the strategies you would use in helping the client to agree on a goal. Describe the basis for your decision.

You work in a community-based agency that works with pregnant and parenting teens who are wards of the state. Graycee is a 17 year old parenting teen. Her six- month old child is not a ward and Graycee is determined to keep her child out of the system. She goes to great lengths to provide for and protect the child. Her greatest fear is that her child will be taken away from her, just like she was taken away from her mother. Having the child sleep with her in the same bed is one of the ways that the client attempts to protect and nurture her child. In an effort to discourage unsafe sleep, your agency gave all of the teen moms portable infant cribs, so that their children could be near them but not in the same bed. During a recent visit, Graycee's child protection caseworker noticed that the crib was still in the box. The caseworker told Graycee that sleeping with the child was dangerous, and unless she used the crib she would make a report which could result in the child being removed from her care. During the visit, the worker wrote a safety goal for Graycee, "Refrain from unsafe sleeping with your child."

You are meeting with Graycee a day after the caseworker's visit. She seems to be extremely agitated and less than happy to see you. When you asked her about the reason for her unusual behavior, she stated, "I am tired of people telling me what to do. My baby is safe! I sleep with my baby because I want to keep him safe. I know other people who sleep with their children, and noting has happened to them."

1. Identify which strategy (or strategies) that you would use in this case and indicate the basis for your decision.

2. Describe the conversation that you would have with Graycee so that she could achieve the goals that the caseworker had set for her.

3. You are somewhat sympathetic to Graycee. You consider whether it would be useful to provide her with information about safe sleeping options, but you are unclear how to proceed. Describe how you would go about gathering information that you could share with Gracycee.

Goal: This exercise is designed to assist you in understanding the reactance of involuntary clients.

Focus Competencies and Practice Behaviors
- EP 2.1.1b Practice personal reflection and self-correction to assure continual professional development
- EP 2.1.2a Recognize and mange personal values in a way the allows for professional values to guide practice
- EP 2.1.7a Utilize a conceptual framework to guide the processes of assessment, intervention, and evaluation
- EP 2.1.10i Implement prevention interventions that enhance client capacity

Invite a classmate to role-play Graycee's case situation with you, in which you take the role of Graycee. Begin the role-play by saying, "I am tired of people in my business."

The classmate, acting as the social worker interacts with you based on the scenario below.

Scenario: Graycee remains agitated and accuses you of working against her, just like everyone else. You think that she is being unfair, and you resent her attitude. If you had a choice, you would avoid cases in which the client is involuntary. It is your opinion that involuntary clients are unwilling to change. Like Graycee, they often blame others for their troubles instead of taking responsibility for their behavior. For this reason, you believe that you have to be firm with them; otherwise they are unlikely to do what they are told to do. With this in mind, you proceed with Graycee based on your beliefs, and assert your authority. You also remind her that as a mandated reporter, you are required to report a situation in which her child is unsafe. You think to yourself the sooner the visit is over, the better you will feel.

Graycee:

1. Describe how you responded to the social worker.

2. Describe your behavioral and emotional reactions to what the social worker said and how you acted.

Social Worker:

1. Describe Graycee's reactive responses to what you said and did

2. Describe the effects that Graycee's reactions had on you and how you responded to Gracie and how you responded.

3. Describe the steps that you could have taken to diffuse and minimize Graycee's reactions.

Social Worker and Graycee:

1. Indicate what the two of you learned about reactance as a result of the role-play.

2. Identify how you would apply your learning to your work with involuntary clients.

3. Describe the steps that you will take in the future in your work with involuntary clients that would uphold your professional responsibility.

Goal: To assist you in distinguishing your role and that of the client in selecting and defining goals.

Focus Competencies or Practice Behaviors
- EP 2.1.1c Attend to professional roles and boundaries
- EP 2.1.10j Help clients solve problems

For each vignette, indicate how you would respond.

Vignette 1: During a session in which you and the client began the process of selecting and defining goals, the client stated, "I don't know what to do; I thought that you would tell me."

Vignette 2: A minor is referred to you by a teacher for "acting out" in class.

Vignette 3: A client has indicated that he is ready to move forward with selecting and defining a specific goal, but his body language seemed to give a different message.

Vignette 4: In a previous session, you and the client agreed that in the next session, you would help her in deciding on a priority goal. The client comes to the session with several members of her family. It is clear that they intended to be involved in the process, but they asked that you explain the purpose and function of goals. Also, they want to know who is involved in the process of developing goals.

Exercise 12.6
Facilitating Goal Decisions with Minors

Goal: To enhance your skills in the process of developing goals with minors.

Focus Competencies and Practice Behaviors
- EP 2.1.10c Develop mutually agreed-on focus of work and desired outcomes
- EP 2.1.10j Help clients solve problems

Review "Applying Goal Development Guidelines with Minors" and indicate what you would do in the case example.

Margie is a 12-year old African American female attending a charter school. She was referred to you by a teacher. In her report, the teacher emphasized that Margie has problems with completing her school work. However, the teacher is hopeful because she believes that Margie is capable of being a good student. She would like for you and Margie to set "improved academic performance" as a goal, because Margie would like to go to college.

1. Describe how you would begin the interview with Margie.

2. What specific information do you need from Margie?

3. What specific information do you need from the teacher?

4. Describe how you would involve Margie in achieving the goal and evaluating her performance.

5. Who else might you involve in helping Margie to improve her academic performance?

6. Describe other factors that you would consider or additional steps that you would take in this case.

Name: _____ Date: _____

Supervisor's Name: _____

Focus Competencies/Practice Behaviors:

- EP 2.1.1b Practice personal reflection and self-correction to assure continual professional development
- EP 2.1.1f Use supervision and consultation
- EP 2.1.1c Attend to professional roles and boundaries
- EP 2.1.2b Recognize and manage personal values in a way that Recognize personal values in that allows for professional values to guide practice
- EP 2.1.7a Utilize a conceptual framework to guide the processes of assessment, intervention, and evaluation
- EP 2.1.10c Develop mutually agreed-on focus of work and desired outcomes
- EP 2.1.10i Implement prevention interventions that enhances client capacities
- EP 2.1.10j Help clients solve problems
- EP 2.1.10m Critically analyze, monitor and evaluate interventions

Instructions: Evaluate your work or your partner's work in the Focus Practice Behaviors by completing the Practice Behaviors Assessment form below. What other Practice Behaviors did you use to complete these Exercises? Be sure to record them in your assessments.

1.	I have attained this competency/practice behavior (in the range of 80 to 100%)
2.	I have largely attained this competency/practice behavior (in the range of 60 to 80%)
3.	I have partially attained this competency/practice behavior (in the range of 40 to 60%)
4.	I have made a little progress in attaining this competency/practice behavior (in the range of 20 to 40%
5.	I have made almost no progress in attaining this competency/practice behavior (in the range of 0 to 20%)

EPAS 2008 Core Competencies & Core Practice Behaviors	Student Self Assessment						Evaluator Feedback
Student and Evaluator Assessment Scale and Comments	0	1	2	3	4	5	Agree/Disagree/Comments
2.1.1 Identity as a Professional Social Worker and Conduct Oneself Accordingly:							
a. Advocate for client access to the services of social work							
b. Practice personal reflection and self-correction to assure continual professional development							
c. Attend to professional roles and boundaries							

d. Demonstrate professional demeanor in behavior, appearance, and communication								
e. Engage in career-long learning								
f. Use supervision and consultation								
2.1.2 Apply Social Work Ethical Principles to Guide Professional Practice:								
a. Recognize and manage personal values in a way that allows professional values to guide practice								
b. Make ethical decisions by applying NASW Code of Ethics and, as applicable, IFSW/IASSW Ethics in Social Work, Statement of Principles								
c. Tolerate ambiguity in resolving ethical conflicts								
d. Apply strategies in resolving ethical conflicts								
2.1.3 Apply Critical Thinking to Inform and Communicate Professional Judgments:								
a. Distinguish, appraise, and integrate multiple sources of knowledge, including research-based knowledge and practice wisdom								
b. Analyze models of assessment, prevention, intervention, and evaluation								
c. Demonstrate effective oral and written communication in working with individuals, families, groups, organizations, communities, and colleagues								
2.1.4 Engage Diversity and Difference in Practice:								
a. Recognize the extent to which a culture's structures and values may oppress, marginalize, alienate, or create or enhance privilege and power								
b. Gain sufficient self-awareness to eliminate the influence of personal biases and values in working with diverse groups								
c. Recognize and communicate their understanding of the importance of difference in shaping life experiences								

d. View themselves as learners and engage those with whom they work as informants							
2.1.5 Advance Human Rights and Social and Economic Justice							
a. Understand forms and mechanisms of oppression and discrimination							
b. Advocate for human rights and social and economic justice							
c. Engage in practices that advance social and economic justice							
2.1.6 Engage in research-informed practice and practice-informed research							
a. Use practice experience to inform scientific inquiry							
b. Use research evidence to inform practice							
2.1.7 Apply knowledge of human behavior and the social environment:							
a. Utilize conceptual frameworks to guide the processes of assessment, intervention, and evaluation							
b. Critique and apply knowledge to understand person and environment							
2.1.8 Engage in policy practice to advance social and economic well-being and to deliver effective social work services:							
a. Analyze, formulate, and advocate for policies that advance social well-being							
b. Collaborate with colleagues and clients for effective policy action							
2.1.9 Respond to contexts that shape practice:							
a. Continuously discover, appraise, and attend to changing locales, populations, scientific and technological developments, and emerging societal trends to provide relevant services							
b. Provide leadership in promoting sustainable changes in service delivery and practice to improve the quality of social services							

2.1.10 Engage, assess, intervene, and evaluate with individuals, families, groups, organizations and communities:							
a. Substantively and affectively prepare for action with individuals, families, groups, organizations, and communities							
b. Use empathy and other interpersonal skills							
c. Develop a mutually agreed-on focus of work and desired outcomes							
d. Collect, organize, and interpret client data							
e. Assess client strengths and limitations							
f. Develop mutually agreed-on intervention goals and objectives							
g. Select appropriate intervention strategies.							
h. Initiate actions to achieve organizational goals							
i. Implement prevention interventions that enhance client capacities							
j. Help clients resolve problems							
k. Negotiate, mediate, and advocate for clients							
l. Facilitate transitions and endings							
m. Critically analyze, monitor, and evaluate interventions							

Exercise 13.1
Really, Tell Me More!

Goal: To assist you in applying critical thinking skills in determining the efficacy of a treatment model.

Focus Competencies and Practice Behaviors

- EP 2.1.2d Apply strategies of ethical reasoning skills to arrive at principled decisions
- EP 2.1.3b Analyze models of assessment, prevention, intervention, and evaluation
- EP 2.1.6b Use of research to inform practice
- EP 2.1.10g Select appropriate intervention strategies

Due to recent demographic shifts in the area of the city in which your agency is located, the client population has become more diverse as has your caseload. Develop a set of questions that you would ask that will help you in determining whether you would include the models below in your work with clients. You work mainly with individuals.

Scenario 1: You are attending a workshop. The enthusiastic workshop leaders present a model that they emphasize as being capable of dramatically changing the practice of the workshop participants with individuals and families, in that it addresses variety of problems. The leaders provide numerous case examples for participants to review and comment. Participants were invited to ask questions at the conclusion of the workshop.

In the space below, identify the 4-6 questions that you would ask the workshop presenters and indicate the basis for your choice of questions.

Question 1:

Question 2:

Question 3:

Question 4:

Question 5:

Question 6:

Identify the research evidence would you seek about the model, and describe the steps that you would take in gathering this information.

| **Exercise 13.2** |
| **It Would Take a Miracle!** |

Goal: This exercise is designed to assist you in applying the techniques and procedures of the Solution-Focused Brief Treatment Approach.

Focus Competencies and Practice Behaviors
- EP 2.17a Utilize conceptual framework to guide the process of assessment, intervention, and evaluation
- EP 2.1.10d Collect and interpret client data
- EP 2.1.10f Develop a mutually agreed-on intervention goals and objectives
- EP 2.1.10g Select appropriate intervention strategies
- EP 2.1.10j Help clients solve problems

Read the case situation, and using the prompts as guides, indicate what you would do and the basis for your decision.

Jamala, age 15, and her mother, Selima, are locked in a conflict about privileges and chores. Selima, a single mother, believes that Jamala should complete all of her daily cleaning chores to her satisfaction before going out with her friends. Previously, Selima had given Jamala a list of the specific behaviors that needed to be changed so that she could regain privileges. Jamala ignored the list, and refused to talk to Selima. Jamala's behavior is another source of tension between the two. Selima sees Jamala's behavior as argumentative, headstrong and disrespectful.

Jamala wants to get her mom off her back. The latest blow-up occurred because Selima refused to allow Jamala to participate in outings with her friends.

As you listened to the two of them, you observed that both seemed to be committed to the blame-game, in that each attributed the reasons for their conflict to each other. As the session ended, Selima stated, "At this point, it would take a miracle for us to be able to get along," and Jamala laughed. Nonetheless, they both agreed to continue to work with you in an effort to resolve their conflicted relationship.

1. Describe the Solution-Focused Brief Treatment approach and your rationale for select the approach in this case.

2. Explain how you would talk to Selima and Jamala about the approach so that you are assured that they are in agreement.

3. As you work with Selima and Jamala, describe how you would use the following questions and the basis for your decision.

   Coping:

   Scaling:

   Exceptions:

   Miracle

4. Jamala and Selima recounted several instances in which their relationship was free of conflict. Develop a post-session formulate task.

5. In a subsequent session, Selima and Jamala reported that their relationship had improved. Describe how you would use a scaling question, and the techniques of complementing and bridging.

6. Identify other Solution-Focused techniques that you would use and additional questions that you would ask in this session.

Goal: To assist you in developing your skills in applying the techniques and procedures of the Task-Centered approach.

Focus Competencies and Practice Behaviors
- EP 2.1.10d Collect and interpret client data
- EP 2.1.10j Help client solve problems
- EP 2.1.10m Critically analyze, monitor, and evaluate interventions

In this exercise, continue with the case example of Selima and Jamala. Following the prompts, describe what you would do.

1. Describe the Task-centered approach to Selima and Jamala.

2. Summarize your understanding of the target problem

3. Write a goal to address the target problem.

4. Develop a general task.

5. Develop specific tasks for the general tasks.

6. Describe how you would determine Selima's and Jamala's commitment to carry out tasks.

7. Describe the details for carrying out individual tasks.

8. Discuss how you would analyze and resolve potential obstacles to tasks completion.

9. Summarize the task plan.

10. Describe how you would conduct an interview with Selima and Jamala which reviews the status of the target problem and their progress toward the goal.

11. In applying the Task-centered approach in this case, discuss other techniques and procedures that you would use, and the basis for your decision.

12. Describe procedures and techniques of the Solution-Focused Brief Treatment approach that you would use with the Task-centered approach, and your rationale.

Exercise 13.4
Responding to Client Beliefs and Self- Statements

Goal: To assist you in developing skills in helping clients in exploring and gaining insights into their problematic beliefs and self-statements.

Focus Competencies and Practice Behaviors
- EP 2.1.7a Apply knowledge of human behavior in the social environment
- EP 2.1.10b Use empathy and other interpersonal skills
- EP 2.1.10i Implement prevention interventions that enhance client capacities
- EP 2.1.10j Help clients solve problems

Each of the scenarios involves a client statement or belief about his or her situation. As the social worker, write a response for each of the scenarios. At the conclusion of the exercise, evaluate your use of empathy and other interpersonal skills, in responding to the client.

Scenario A: Elderly client concerned about visits from her daughter: "There's no point in my asking my daughter to visit me more often. She will just see my asking her as an attempt to get attention and trying to embarrass her. I'm afraid to say anything for fear she will stop visiting me at all. After all, she is busy with her own family."

Social Worker Response:

Scenario B: Student Preparing for Exam: **"**I've got to study every available minute, because I am not a very good student. Next week I have a test, and if I don't get the highest score possible, it will just be awful."

Social Worker Response:

Scenario C: Relative Caring for Children: "I don't want to care for my sister's children. I don't want to upset her. She should understand that I have a life too. But because I am single, she thinks that I should be available."

Social Worker Response:

Scenario D: Elderly client refusing to go to the Doctor: "I' m not going back to that doctor. Every time I go there, he wants to draw blood. What is need my blood for, maybe so he can get Medicaid and Medicare money, makes me sick how dishonest some people can be. I know about these doctors and how they experiment on poor black people."

Social Worker Response:

Review your responses: Identify and evaluate your use of empathy and other interpersonal skills.

Exercise 13.6
Case Management Plan

Goal: To assist you in developing a coordinated case plan.

Focus Competencies and Practice Behaviors
- EP 2.1.10f Develop a mutually agreed-on intervention goals and objectives
- EP 2.1.10j Help clients solve problems

You are a case manager in a shelter for homeless and runaway youth. The goal of the shelter is assist the youth in becoming independent. Using the prompts as guides, complete the tasks and describe what you would do.

Justin, age 17 is homeless. He became homeless when he came out to his family. Immediately his father ordered him out of the house. Prior to moving into the shelter, Justin had couch-surfed with friends. He'd also slept under bridges, in an adult shelter, and in an abandoned house with other homeless youth. In addition to needing a permanent place to live, Justin has a number of medical problems that need attention.

1. As the case manager for Justin, describe your role and responsibilities.

2. Develop a summary of assessed needs.

3. Describe a goal for each need.

4. Develop a case plan that includes coordinated referral resources foe Justin, using the illustrated Figure 13-5 in Chapter 13.

Goals   Providers   Sessions/Duration   Monitoring   Evaluation/Reassessment.

5. Review the case plan, and discuss is required of you in developing, coordinating and evaluating the plan.

Chapter 13
Competencies/Practice Behaviors Exercises Assessment:

Name: _____ **Date:** _____
Supervisor's Name: _____

Focus Competencies/Practice Behaviors:
- EP 2.1.2d Apply strategies of ethical reasoning skills to arrive at principled decisions
- EP 2.1.3b Analyze models of assessment, prevention, intervention, and evaluation
- EP 2.1.7a Utilize conceptual framework to guide process of assessment, intervention, and evaluation
- EP 2.1.7b Apply knowledge of human behavior in the social environment
- EP 1.1.10b Use empathy and other interpersonal skills
- EP 2.1.10d Collect, organize and interpret client data
- EP 2.1.10f Develop mutually agreed-on intervention goals and objectives
- EP 2.1.10g Select appropriate intervention strategies
- EP 2.1.10j Help clients solve problems
- EP 2.1.10i Implement prevention interventions that enhance client capacities
- EP 2.1.10m Critically analyze, monitor, and evaluate interventions

Instructions: Evaluate your work or your partner's work in the Focus Practice Behaviors by completing the Practice Behaviors Assessment form below. What other Practice Behaviors did you use to complete these Exercises? Be sure to record them in your assessments.

1.	I have attained this competency/practice behavior (in the range of 80 to 100%)
2.	I have largely attained this competency/practice behavior (in the range of 60 to 80%)
3.	I have partially attained this competency/practice behavior (in the range of 40 to 60%)
4.	I have made a little progress in attaining this competency/practice behavior (in the range of 20 to 40%
5.	I have made almost no progress in attaining this competency/practice behavior (in the range of 0 to 20%)

EPAS 2008 Core Competencies & Core Practice Behaviors	Student Self Assessment						Evaluator Feedback
Student and Evaluator Assessment Scale and Comments	0	1	2	3	4	5	Agree/Disagree/Comments
2.1.1 Identity as a Professional Social Worker and Conduct Oneself Accordingly:							
a. Advocate for client access to the services of social work							
b. Practice personal reflection and self-correction to assure continual professional development							
c. Attend to professional roles and boundaries							

- 152 -

d. Demonstrate professional demeanor in behavior, appearance, and communication								
e. Engage in career-long learning								
f. Use supervision and consultation								
2.1.2 Apply Social Work Ethical Principles to Guide Professional Practice:								
a. Recognize and manage personal values in a way that allows professional values to guide practice								
b. Make ethical decisions by applying NASW Code of Ethics and, as applicable, IFSW/IASSW Ethics in Social Work, Statement of Principles								
c. Tolerate ambiguity in resolving ethical conflicts								
d. Apply strategies in resolving ethical conflicts								
2.1.3 Apply Critical Thinking to Inform and Communicate Professional Judgments:								
a. Distinguish, appraise, and integrate multiple sources of knowledge, including research-based knowledge and practice wisdom								
b. Analyze models of assessment, prevention, intervention, and evaluation								
c. Demonstrate effective oral and written communication in working with individuals, families, groups, organizations, communities, and colleagues								
2.1.4 Engage Diversity and Difference in Practice:								
a. Recognize the extent to which a culture's structures and values may oppress, marginalize, alienate, or create or enhance privilege and power								
b. Gain sufficient self-awareness to eliminate the influence of personal biases and values in working with diverse groups								
c. Recognize and communicate their understanding of the importance of difference in shaping life experiences								

d. View themselves as learners and engage those with whom they work as informants							

2.1.5 Advance Human Rights and Social and Economic Justice

a. Understand forms and mechanisms of oppression and discrimination							
b. Advocate for human rights and social and economic justice							
c. Engage in practices that advance social and economic justice							

2.1.6 Engage in research-informed practice and practice-informed research

a. Use practice experience to inform scientific inquiry							
b. Use research evidence to inform practice							

2.1.7 Apply knowledge of human behavior and the social environment:

a. Utilize conceptual frameworks to guide the processes of assessment, intervention, and evaluation							
b. Critique and apply knowledge to understand person and environment							

2.1.8 Engage in policy practice to advance social and economic well-being and to deliver effective social work services:

a. Analyze, formulate, and advocate for policies that advance social well-being							
b. Collaborate with colleagues and clients for effective policy action							

2.1.9 Respond to contexts that shape practice:

a. Continuously discover, appraise, and attend to changing locales, populations, scientific and technological developments, and emerging societal trends to provide relevant services							
b. Provide leadership in promoting sustainable changes in service delivery and practice to improve the quality of social services							

2.1.10 Engage, assess, intervene, and evaluate with individuals, families, groups, organizations and communities:							
a. Substantively and affectively prepare for action with individuals, families, groups, organizations, and communities							
b. Use empathy and other interpersonal skills							
c. Develop a mutually agreed-on focus of work and desired outcomes							
d. Collect, organize, and interpret client data							
e. Assess client strengths and limitations							
f. Develop mutually agreed-on intervention goals and objectives							
g. Select appropriate intervention strategies.							
h. Initiate actions to achieve organizational goals							
i. Implement prevention interventions that enhance client capacities							
j. Help clients resolve problems							
k. Negotiate, mediate, and advocate for clients							
l. Facilitate transitions and endings							
m. Critically analyze, monitor, and evaluate interventions							

Exercise 14.1
What Would You Do?

Goal: This exercise is designed to assist you in understanding the steps involved in social action and advocacy.

Focus Competencies or Practice Behaviors:
- EP 2.1.1a Advocate for client assess to services
- EP 2.1.4a Recognize the extent to which a culture's structures and values may oppress, marginalize, alienate, or create or enhance privilege and power
- EP 2.1.5a Understand the forms and mechanism of oppression and discrimination
- EP 2.1.5b Advocate for human rights and social and economic justice
- EP 2.1.8a Analyze, formulate, and advocate for policies that advance social well-being
- EP 2.1.9b Provide leadership in promoting sustainable changes in service delivery and practice to improve the quality of services
- EP 2.1.10a Substantively and effectively prepare for action with individuals, families, groups organizations and communities.
- EP 2.1.10d Collect and organize client data
- EP 2.1.10g Select appropriate intervention strategy

Read the following case situation and decide upon a course of action.

You are a social worker at the Senior Resource Center which serves a community in which the majority of the residents are poor, minority, and elderly. Several community residents have appealed to you to help them respond to a decision by the transportation authority to relocate the bus stops in their community. Speaking on behalf of other residents, they expressed two concerns: the number of bus stops had been reduced, and the new location was less accessible.

Previously residents had access to several stops along a major street. As a result of the change, there is only one bus stop, which is located in an isolated area on a little-used back street at the bottom of a hill where there are few houses. Because of physical limitations, many of the residents are unable to walk up and down the hill's steep incline, and a significant number were fearful about waiting for a bus in a sparsely populated area.

The relocation of the bus stops came as a surprise to the community. The center had not received information about the move, either. Had you and other center staff been aware of the proposed change, the agency would have mounted a proactive response that included the community. After making numerous phone calls to the city's public transportation office, the official that you spoke to justified the bus relocation as an economic necessity. Further, he stated that "there had been little response from the residents." When asked what information had been provided to the community, he advised that electronic messages had been sent to e-mail addresses that residents had provided to his office, but he was uncertain of the number. In addition, an announcement had been posted to the classified section of a major daily newspaper.

Approximately 80% of the community residents relied on public transit for their transportation needs. Because the bus service also connected to the light rail, they were able to do their grocery shopping, participate in activities at the senior center and attend church. Therefore the decision would make a significant difference in the mobility of the residents.

1. Following the prompts analyze and comment on the issues in this situation related to:

Power:

Equality:

Electronic communication:

Newspaper Communication:

Additional issues that you may have identified:

Although the decision about the bus service is in the works, in two weeks, a final public response meeting is planned. In preparation for this meeting, your supervisor asked you look into the situation and to make a recommendation to the agency's administrative group about how the agency should respond based on the information that you have gathered. You agreed to do so, as you and other staff believed that the center should act with and on behalf of the community.

After each of the numbered prompts state your proposed recommendation and the rationale.

1. Describe your recommendation:

2. Describe the methods that you used to collect information that formed the basis for your recommendation, and your rationale for .

3. Describe the intervention proposed and your rationale:

4. How will you implement intervention strategy? What is your rationale for the strategy?

5. List the potential challenges you'll face. Why?

6. How will you evaluate the effectiveness of the intervention? Describe your rationale for the evaluation method.

Exercise 14.2
Organizing a Response to a Proposed Policy That Will Have a Disparate
Impact on a Segment of a Client Population

Goal: This exercise is designed to assist you in understanding the ways in which you can respond to a policy that is likely to result in unequal access to needed services for clients.

Focus Competencies and Practice Behaviors
- EP 2.1.1a Advocate for client access to services
- EP 2.1.5a Advocate for human rights and social and economic justice.
- EP 2.1.8a Analyze, formulate, and advocate for policies that advance social well-being

Read the scenario and answer the questions. In addition, you may wish to develop other questions.

You are working at a community-based mental health center as a case manager for adults who have schizophrenia and other serious mental illnesses. Many of the clients on your case load are people of color who use Social Security Disability Income or Supplemental Security Income to meet their basic needs. Recently, the governor of your state proposed cutbacks in medical assistance for low-income persons, including the elimination of dental care benefits for adults with disabilities. Many of your clients need routine dental care, and many also need eye glasses. What might you do in response to the proposed cuts by the governor,?

Using the prompts as a guide, answer the following questions.

1. How will you gather information to understand the possible impact of the proposed cut for adult with disabilities?

2. Describe how will you educate your clients about the proposed cuts in the services that they receive?

3. Identify other resources in the community that might be willing to respond to the governor's proposal?

4. What kinds of community organization could you collaborate with in responding to the proposal, and in advocating for the clients?

5. Add your own questions or thoughts about organizing a response.

Policy Advocacy Worksheet
Exercise 14.3

Goal: This exercise is designed to assist you in analyzing the extent that public policy influences your work with clients.

Focus Competencies or Practice Behaviors:
- EP 2.1.8a Analyze, formulate, and advocate for policies that advance social well-being

Complete this exercise by answering the following questions:

1. Identify one public policy that is having a significant impact on your work or on the people you work with?

2. What special or first-hand knowledge do you have regarding the impact of the policy that you could share with an elected official?

3. What is one coalition or advocacy group from which you could get strategic information about the impact of the public policy?

4. What steps could you take to mobilize others in your workplace or community around the public policy?

5. What more do you need to learn in order to become an effective policy advocate?

Goal: To assist you in organizing information that you would present to an elected official about the impact that a policy has on clients.

Focus Competencies or Practice Behaviors:

- EP 2.1.8a Analyze, formulate, and advocate for policies that advance social well-being

Ask a peer to join you in a role-play conversation with an elected official in which you would share information about the impact of the public policy on your clients and your work. Have the peer act in the role of the elected official. In the space below, outline your 3-4 talking points.

1. Talking Points

2. Upon completion of the role-play, evaluate your effort.

   a. What were your expectations of the conversation with the elected official?

   b. How did the public official react?

   c. How did you think that you did in presenting information about the public policy?

   d. Ask the peer for feedback to provide.

Goal: To assist you in preparing for planning and developing resources for a specific population.

Focus Practice Competencies and Practice Behaviors
- EP 2.1.10b Use empathy and other interpersonal skills
- EP 2.1.4d View themselves as learners and engage those with whom that work as key informants
- EP 2.1.6b Use research evidence to inform practice
- EP 2.1.10a Substantively and effectively prepare for action with individuals, families, groups, communities and organizations
- EP 2.1.10d Collect and organize client data
- EP 2.1.10e Assess client strengths and limitations
- EP 2.1.10h Initiate action to achieve organizational goals

Read the situation below. Invite a peer partner to complete this exercise with you. Following the prompts, reach an agreement in how the two of you would proceed.

Over a two-year period the client population served by your agency has dramatically changed. While the agency's administrative team is concerned about the service implications related to the demographic shift, at this point in time they are unsure about how to respond. In a recent staff meeting the issue of providing appropriate services to the largest number of newcomers in a specific geographical area was discussed at length. Nonetheless, a majority of staff believed that the agency lacked sufficient information to plan and develop services.

You are considered to be most familiar with the changing community because much of your work is community-based. You were asked to partner with another staff person to explore the service needs. The information that the two of you provide will be included in the agency's annual strategic plan.

1. Describe how you would gather information and document the resource needs or the group and include the method (s) that you would use.

2. As you gather information, discuss the specific skills that you would use.

   a. Interpersonal:

   b. Communication:

   c. Analysis:

3. Describe how you would assess the strengths and limitations of the community.

4. Discuss whether or not you talk to agency staff, and the basis of your decision.

5. Assuming that you have decided to interview agency staff, what questions would you ask and why?

6. Planning and developing resources for the population can result in benefits and also risks to the agency. Identify both the benefits and risks:

7. As you reviewed the interviews that you conducted with staff, you noted two reoccurring themes. Specifically staff had reservations about whether they had sufficient knowledge and skills to serve the group, and a significant number of agency staff also thought that the most viable solution was for the agency to hire individuals from the same group to work with the clients. How would you respond?

   a. Staff reservations about their knowledge and skill:

   b. Hiring individuals from the group to work with the specific population:

Goal: This exercise is designed to help you in understanding the importance of respecting clients' dignity and worth.

Focus Competencies and Practice Behaviors:
- EP 2.1.1d Demonstrate professional demeanor in behavior, appearance and communication
- EP 2.1.10b Use empathy and other interpersonal skills
- EP 2.1.2d Apply strategies of ethical decision-making

You are employed as a case manager with an agency that provides financial support and family-based services to families in poverty in your city. Your agency's food shelf has been particularly impacted by recent natural disasters in the area that have increased demand for financial and food assistance. You want to develop a base of resources for food assistance for this area of the city, and you want to ensure that those with the greatest needs are helped first. There are a few families who you and other staff believe are scamming the system. For instance, a colleague reported during a staff meeting that she recently observed the father in one family buying ice cream at the local convenience store. In addition, several people laughed when another staff person said, "The entire family needs to be on a diet." Even though the comments made you uncomfortable, you refrained from saying anything.

The guidelines in the resource plan that you developed include a provision that all people are to be served during this difficult period, without having to document their need. The plan was adopted by the agency, although some staff expressed reservations that an open door plan would invite abuse.

As you walked through the agency's waiting area for a second time, you noticed that the mother of the family and four children seemed to have been waiting for a lengthy period of time. This particular family had been discussed in the staff meeting where some staff had made disparaging remarks. When you inquired of the receptionist about how long the mother had been waiting, she informed you that she had been told to have the mother wait until all other clients had been served. As you approached the mother to talk to her about what she needed, she looked embarrassed and began to cry.

1. Identify the ethical issues in this scenario.

2. What would you say to the mother in order to ease her discomfort?

3. What are the attitudes and behaviors on your part and that of other staff that showed a lack of respect for this family?

4. Reflect upon what you would do, should you observe similar treatment of clients in future situations.

Chapter 14
Competencies/Practice Behaviors Exercises Assessment:

Name: _____ **Date:** _____

Supervisor's Name: _____

Focus Competencies/Practice Behaviors:

- EP 2.1.1a Advocate for client access to services
- EP 2.1.1d Demonstrate professional demeanor in behavior, appearance and communication
- EP 2.1.4b Gain sufficient self-awareness to eliminate the influence of personal biases and values in working with diverse groups
- EP 2.1.4d View themselves as learners and engage those with whom that work as key informants
- EP 2.1.5a Understand the forms and mechanism of oppression and discrimination
- EP 2.1.5b Advocate for human rights and social and economic justice.
- EP 2.1.6b Use research evidence to inform practice
- EP 2.1.8a Analyze, formulate, and advocate for policies that advance social well-being
- EP 2.1.9b Provide leadership in promoting sustainable changes in service delivery and practice to improve the quality of services
- EP 2.1.10a Substantively and effectively prepare for action with individuals, families, groups, communities and organizations
- EP 2.1.10b Use empathy and other interpersonal skills
- EP 2.1.10d Collect and organize client data

- EP 2.1.10e Assess client strengths and limitation
- EP 2.1.10h Initiate action to achieve organizational goals
- EP 2.1.10g Select appropriate intervention strategy
- EP 2.1.2d Apply strategies of ethical decision-making

Instructions: Evaluate your work or your partner's work in the Focus Practice Behaviors by completing the Practice Behaviors Assessment form below. What other Practice Behaviors did you use to complete these Exercises? Be sure to record them in your assessments.

1.	I have attained this competency/practice behavior (in the range of 80 to 100%)
2.	I have largely attained this competency/practice behavior (in the range of 60 to 80%)
3.	I have partially attained this competency/practice behavior (in the range of 40 to 60%)
4.	I have made a little progress in attaining this competency/practice behavior (in the range of 20 to 40%
5.	I have made almost no progress in attaining this competency/practice behavior (in the range of 0 to 20%)

EPAS 2008 Core Competencies & Core Practice Behaviors	Student Self Assessment						Evaluator Feedback
Student and Evaluator Assessment Scale and Comments	0	1	2	3	4	5	Agree/Disagree/Comments
2.1.1 Identity as a Professional Social Worker and Conduct Oneself Accordingly:							
a. Advocate for client access to the services of social work							
b. Practice personal reflection and self-correction to assure continual professional development							
c. Attend to professional roles and boundaries							
d. Demonstrate professional demeanor in behavior, appearance, and communication							
e. Engage in career-long learning							
f. Use supervision and consultation							
2.1.2 Apply Social Work Ethical Principles to Guide Professional Practice:							
a. Recognize and manage personal values in a way that allows professional values to guide practice							
b. Make ethical decisions by applying NASW Code of Ethics and, as applicable, IFSW/IASSW Ethics in Social Work, Statement of Principles							
c. Tolerate ambiguity in resolving ethical conflicts							
d. Apply strategies in resolving ethical conflicts							
2.1.3 Apply Critical Thinking to Inform and Communicate Professional Judgments:							
a. Distinguish, appraise, and integrate multiple sources of knowledge, including research-based knowledge and practice wisdom							
b. Analyze models of assessment, prevention, intervention, and evaluation							
c. Demonstrate effective oral and written communication in working with individuals, families, groups, organizations, communities, and colleagues							

2.1.4 Engage Diversity and Difference in Practice:								
a. Recognize the extent to which a culture's structures and values may oppress, marginalize, alienate, or create or enhance privilege and power								
b. Gain sufficient self-awareness to eliminate the influence of personal biases and values in working with diverse groups								
c. Recognize and communicate their understanding of the importance of difference in shaping life experiences								
d. View themselves as learners and engage those with whom they work as informants								
2.1.5 Advance Human Rights and Social and Economic Justice								
a. Understand forms and mechanisms of oppression and discrimination								
b. Advocate for human rights and social and economic justice								
c. Engage in practices that advance social and economic justice								
2.1.6 Engage in research-informed practice and practice-informed research								
a. Use practice experience to inform scientific inquiry								
b. Use research evidence to inform practice								
2.1.7 Apply knowledge of human behavior and the social environment:								
a. Utilize conceptual frameworks to guide the processes of assessment, intervention, and evaluation								
b. Critique and apply knowledge to understand person and environment								
2.1.8 Engage in policy practice to advance social and economic well-being and to deliver effective social work services:								
a. Analyze, formulate, and advocate for policies that advance social well-being								
b. Collaborate with colleagues and clients for effective policy action								

2.1.9 Respond to contexts that shape practice:							
a. Continuously discover, appraise, and attend to changing locales, populations, scientific and technological developments, and emerging societal trends to provide relevant services							
b. Provide leadership in promoting sustainable changes in service delivery and practice to improve the quality of social services							
2.1.10 Engage, assess, intervene, and evaluate with individuals, families, groups, organizations and communities:							
a. Substantively and affectively prepare for action with individuals, families, groups, organizations, and communities							
b. Use empathy and other interpersonal skills							
c. Develop a mutually agreed-on focus of work and desired outcomes							
d. Collect, organize, and interpret client data							
e. Assess client strengths and limitations							
f. Develop mutually agreed-on intervention goals and objectives							
g. Select appropriate intervention strategies.							
h. Initiate actions to achieve organizational goals							
i. Implement prevention interventions that enhance client capacities							
j. Help clients resolve problems							
k. Negotiate, mediate, and advocate for clients							
l. Facilitate transitions and endings							
m. Critically analyze, monitor, and evaluate interventions							

Exercise 15.1
Conducting the Initial Family Session

Goal: This exercise is designed to assist you in conducting the initial family session.

Focus Competencies and Practice Behaviors
- EP 2.1.7a Utilize a conceptual framework to guide the process of assessment, intervention, and evaluation
- EP 2.1.10a Substantively and effectively prepare for action with individuals, families, group, communities and organizations
- EP 2.1.10b Use empathy and other interpersonal skills
- EP 2.1.10c Develop mutually agreed-on work focus and desired outcomes
- EP 2.1.10e Assess client strengths and limitations
- EP 2.1.10d Collect, organize and interpret client data

The case involves Mr. and Mrs. Franklin and their 16-year-old son, Kevin.

The objectives to be accomplished in the initial session are illustrated in your text in Table 15-1, *Orchestrating The Initial Family or Couple Session*. For this exercise, specific objectives found in the table are indicated. At the conclusion of the exercise, identify the specific interpersonal and communication skills that you would use in the session and the basis for your decision.

Mr. Franklin began the session with an emphatic statement, "In all of my days, I have never seen a child like this one (pointing to Kevin). He talks back and he's lazy and disrespectful to me and his mother. His teachers are constantly calling the house about his behavior. He could be smart if he applied himself to his school work. No, that's not his way." At that point, Mrs. Franklin interrupted Mr. Franklin, but he talked over her. He said to her, "I know you don't like me telling the truth about him, you're want to make and excuse for him, just as you always do." At that point, Kevin, who had not attempted to speak, glared at his father.

"Now, let me finish my piece," Mr. Franklin, continued, "His way is playing video games and text messaging his friends all hours of the night. The wife and I raised three older children who are successful and living on their own with good jobs. They all followed the rules. Not one was a bit of trouble. He's the last one, and a big disappointment. The wife wanted us to come here, but, I'm done talking. I'm just a working class Joe, and I don't understand what meeting with you is going to change. Either he goes or I do. The phone call from the police was the last straw." Mr. Franklin then sat back in his chair, with his arms across his chest.

Describe how you conduct the family session to:

1. Clarify expectations and explore reservations about the helping process, including potential dynamics of minority status and culture

2. Elicit the family's perception of the problem:

3. Identify the wants and needs of family members:

4. Define the problem as a family problem:

5. Emphasize family strengths:

6. Ask questions to elicit information about patterned behaviors of the family:

7. Begin to assist family members to relate to one another in more positive ways:

8. Establish individual and family goals or solutions:

9. Gauge the motivation of family members to have future sessions and negotiate a contract:

10. Finally, using specific examples identify the interpersonal and communications skills that you would use in the session and the basis for your decision:

Exercise 15.2	
Intervening with the Franklin Family	

Goal: This exercise is designed to assist you in making a decision about a strategy or strategies for intervening with families.

Focus Competencies and Practice Behaviors

- EP 2.1.7a Utilize conceptual framework to guide assessment, intervention, and evaluation
- EP 2.1.10a Substantively and effectively prepares for action with individuals, families, groups, communities and organizations
- EP 2.1.10b Use empathy and other interpersonal skills
- EP 2.1.10d Collect, organize and interpret client data
- EP 2.1.10f Develop mutually agreed-on intervention goals and objectives
- EP 2.1.10j Help clients solve problems

This exercise continues with the case of the Franklin family. Summarize the issues and relational dynamics that are present in the case example. Then based on the identified issues and dynamics, indicate the intervention strategy or strategies that you would use with the family, and the basis for your decision. Add observations, comments or questions that you have about the case and reflect on how you would use this information or seek answers to your questions in a future session with the family.

1. Summary of issues and dynamics

2. Proposed intervention strategy or strategies to address the issues or dynamics that you identified, and the basis for your decision

3. Describe how you would discuss the goals and expected outcomes of the proposed strategy or strategies with the family.

4. Additional observations, comments or questions.

   a. Observations:

   b. Comments:

   c. Questions:

   d. Reflections:

Exercise 15.3
I Have to Visit, But!

Goal: To assist you in recognizing and resolving your discomfort in situations in which safety is a concern.

Focus Competencies and Practice Behaviors

- EP 2.1.1d Demonstrate professional demeanor in behavior, appearance and communication
- EP 2.1.4b Gain sufficient self-awareness to eliminate the influence of personal biases and values in working with diverse groups
- EP2.1.7b Critique and apply knowledge of human behavior in the social environment

Following the prompts, discuss how you would address the situation described in the scenario.

You are a community-based social worker and much of your work involves meeting with clients in their homes. The majority of your clients live in a low-income housing complex. In the neighborhood, police sirens are ever present, as are groups of individuals who appear to be just hanging around in the complex hallways and on the adjacent street corners. Today, you are visiting with a client with whom you have a good working relationship. Even so, you don't particularly like going to his home. Getting to the client's apartment means walking through what your coworkers have characterized as walking a gauntlet. You don't necessarily agree with your coworkers, but you are concerned about how to manage getting to the client's apartment. During previous visits, there have been instances in which individuals have made inappropriate comments that caused you to feel uncomfortable and anxious about your safety.

1. Identify your concerns and indicate whether or not you perceived the encounters and comments as threats.

2. Rate each of the concerns that you identified, using a scale of low (1) to high (5), and indicate the basis for your rating.

3. Discuss the steps that you would take to resolve your discomfort and concerns in a manner that are consistent with your professional role and responsibilities.

4. Describe what you learned about yourself in completing this exercise, including your strengths and indicate areas for your future development.

Exercise 15.4
Home for the Holidays, Part 1

Goal: To assist you in applying a specific intervention technique in helping clients in modifying patterns of interactions.

Focus Competencies and Practice Behaviors
- EP 2.1.7a Utilize conceptual frameworks to guide the process of assessment, intervention, and evaluation
- EP 2.1.10j Help clients solve problems

Invite a classmate to view the video segment of "Home for the Holidays, Part 1," featuring Jackie and Anna. Together, answer the questions that follow. Before watching the video you may find it useful to review content related to content and process levels of family interactions and communication styles discussed in Chapter 10, *Assessing Family Functioning in Diverse and Cultural Contexts*.

In viewing the segment, you and your classmate are looking for how Kim, the social worker, guided the couple in engaging in more effective ways of communication using the technique of On-the-Spot Intervention.

1. Describe the specific problematic interactions and communication patterns for which Kim used the technique as an intervention in assisting Jackie and Anna to communicate in a more constructive manner.

2. Describe the guidelines that Kim followed in implementing the technique

3. Discuss the foundation of the theoretical framework and goals of the intervention.

4. Based on the theoretical framework that you identified, describe other techniques that you would use to improve communications between Jackie and Anna.

Exercise 15.5
Improving Family Alignments and Relationships

Goal: To assist you in helping client to increasing their awareness of family alliances that can cause conflict in their relationships.

Focus Competencies and Practice Behaviors
- EP2.1.10d Collect, organize and interpret client data
- EP 2.1.10e Assess client strengths and limitations
- EP 2.1.10f Develop mutually agreed-on intervention goals and objectives
- EP 2.1.10j Help clients solve problems

View the video segment, entitled "Adolescent Parent and Foster Mother, Part 2," featuring Twanna, the adolescent parent, and Janet, the foster mother.

Following the prompts, complete the tasks indicated.

1. Identify and describe the alignments between the members of the family in this case.

   _____ is aligned with _____

   _____ is aligned with _____

   _____ is aligned with _____

2. Within these alliances, discuss which members of the family seem to have bonds that are:

   a. Weak or uncertain:

   b. Strong:

   c. Tentative:

3. Describe the way in which the bonds have caused problematic interactions between family members.

4. Discuss how you would present the information to the family and involve them in considering their alignments.

5. Describe the intervention steps that you would use in assisting the family to strengthen the bonds and in improving their relationships with each other.

6. Describe the strengths in the family.

Goal: To assist you in enhancing your skills in assisting clients to modify problematic communication and interactions with family members.

Focus Competencies and Practice Behaviors
- EP 2.1.7a Utilize conceptual frameworks to guide the process of assessment, intervention, and evaluation
- EP 2.1.10j Help clients solve problems

View the video "Home for the Holidays, Part 2," which is a follow-up session with Jackie and Anna. In "Home for the Holidays, Part 1" Jackie and Anna were struggling with how to act and be accepted as a couple during a holiday visit with Jackie's family. At the conclusion of the first session Jackie and Anna agreed to a goal of improving their relationship by changing the ways in which they communicated with each other.

Following prompts complete the tasks and answer the questions indicated.

1. Describe how Kim began the session.

2. Describe how Kim coached or assisted Anna and Jackie in improving the communication skills by having them engage in:

    a. Using "I" messages:

    b. Giving and Receiving Positive Feedback:

    c. Developing positive cognitions:

    d. Recognizing communication barriers

    e. Disengaging from conflict:

    f. Focusing on the Future:

g. Understanding differences in communication styles:

h. Developing an agreement for reciprocal change:

3. Summarize the session and what was accomplished.

Chapter 15
Competencies/Practice Behaviors Exercises Assessment:

Name: _____ Date: _____

Supervisor's Name: _____

Focus Competencies/Practice Behaviors:

- EP 2.1.1d Demonstrate professional demeanor in behavior, appearance, and communication
- EP 2.1.4b Gain sufficient self-awareness to eliminate the influence of personal biases and values in working with diverse groups
- EP 2.1.7a Utilize conceptual framework to guide assessment, intervention, and evaluation
- EP 2.1.76b Critique and apply knowledge to understand person and environment
- EP 2.1.10a Substantively and effectively prepare for action with individuals, families, groups, communities and organizations
- EP 2.1.10b Use empathy and other interpersonal skills
- EP 2.1.10c Develop a mutually agreed-on focus of work and desired outcomes
- EP 2.1.10d Collect, organize and interpret client data
- EP 2.1.10e Assess client strengths and limitations
- EP 2.1.10f Develop mutually agreed-on intervention goals and objectives
- EP 2.1.10 Help clients solve problems

Instructions: Evaluate your work or your partner's work in the Focus Practice Behaviors by completing the Practice Behaviors Assessment form below. What other Practice Behaviors did you use to complete these Exercises? Be sure to record them in your assessments.

1.	I have attained this competency/practice behavior (in the range of 80 to 100%)
2.	I have largely attained this competency/practice behavior (in the range of 60 to 80%)
3.	I have partially attained this competency/practice behavior (in the range of 40 to 60%)
4.	I have made a little progress in attaining this competency/practice behavior (in the range of 20 to 40%
5.	I have made almost no progress in attaining this competency/practice behavior (in the range of 0 to 20%)

EPAS 2008 Core Competencies & Core Practice Behaviors	Student Self Assessment						Evaluator Feedback
Student and Evaluator Assessment Scale and Comments	0	1	2	3	4	5	Agree/Disagree/Comments
2.1.1 Identity as a Professional Social Worker and Conduct Oneself Accordingly:							
a. Advocate for client access to the services of social work							
b. Practice personal reflection and self-correction to assure continual professional development							
c. Attend to professional roles and boundaries							

d. Demonstrate professional demeanor in behavior, appearance, and communication								
e. Engage in career-long learning								
f. Use supervision and consultation								
2.1.2 Apply Social Work Ethical Principles to Guide Professional Practice:								
a. Recognize and manage personal values in a way that allows professional values to guide practice								
b. Make ethical decisions by applying NASW Code of Ethics and, as applicable, IFSW/IASSW Ethics in Social Work, Statement of Principles								
c. Tolerate ambiguity in resolving ethical conflicts								
d. Apply strategies in resolving ethical conflicts								
2.1.3 Apply Critical Thinking to Inform and Communicate Professional Judgments:								
a. Distinguish, appraise, and integrate multiple sources of knowledge, including research-based knowledge and practice wisdom								
b. Analyze models of assessment, prevention, intervention, and evaluation								
c. Demonstrate effective oral and written communication in working with individuals, families, groups, organizations, communities, and colleagues								
2.1.4 Engage Diversity and Difference in Practice:								
a. Recognize the extent to which a culture's structures and values may oppress, marginalize, alienate, or create or enhance privilege and power								
b. Gain sufficient self-awareness to eliminate the influence of personal biases and values in working with diverse groups								
c. Recognize and communicate their understanding of the importance of difference in shaping life experiences								
d. View themselves as learners and engage those with whom they work as informants								

2.1.5 Advance Human Rights and Social and Economic Justice							
a. Understand forms and mechanisms of oppression and discrimination							
b. Advocate for human rights and social and economic justice							
c. Engage in practices that advance social and economic justice							
2.1.6 Engage in research-informed practice and practice-informed research							
a. Use practice experience to inform scientific inquiry							
b. Use research evidence to inform practice							
2.1.7 Apply knowledge of human behavior and the social environment:							
a. Utilize conceptual frameworks to guide the processes of assessment, intervention, and evaluation							
b. Critique and apply knowledge to understand person and environment							
2.1.8 Engage in policy practice to advance social and economic well-being and to deliver effective social work services:							
a. Analyze, formulate, and advocate for policies that advance social well-being							
b. Collaborate with colleagues and clients for effective policy action							
2.1.9 Respond to contexts that shape practice:							
a. Continuously discover, appraise, and attend to changing locales, populations, scientific and technological developments, and emerging societal trends to provide relevant services							
b. Provide leadership in promoting sustainable changes in service delivery and practice to improve the quality of social services							
2.1.10 Engage, assess, intervene, and evaluate with individuals, families, groups, organizations and communities:							
a. Substantively and affectively prepare for action with individuals, families, groups, organizations, and communities							
b. Use empathy and other interpersonal skills							
c. Develop a mutually agreed-on focus of work and desired outcomes							

d. Collect, organize, and interpret client data							
e. Assess client strengths and limitations							
f. Develop mutually agreed-on intervention goals and objectives							
g. Select appropriate intervention strategies.							
h. Initiate actions to achieve organizational goals							
i. Implement prevention interventions that enhance client capacities							
j. Help clients resolve problems							
k. Negotiate, mediate, and advocate for clients							
l. Facilitate transitions and endings							
m. Critically analyze, monitor, and evaluate interventions							

Chapter 16
Intervening in Social Work Groups

Exercise 16.1
The Phases of Groups

Goal: To increase understanding of group phases by applying them to past or current group experiences.

Focus Competencies or Practice Behaviors:
- EP 2.1.7a Utilize conceptual frameworks to guide the processes of assessment, intervention, and evaluation
- EP 2.1.10a Substantively and affectively prepare for action with individuals, families, groups, organizations, and communities
- EP 2.1.10l Facilitate transitions and endings

Select a group in which you have been or are a member. These may include classes, clubs, group assignments, sorority or fraternity, teams, committees, support or therapy groups, or groups organized around hobbies, interests, politics or faith communities.

For each of the following questions address the degree to which your group did or did not conform to the characteristics expected at that stage. If you believe your group did reflect the developmental features of the stage, provide examples of the behaviors that support your conclusion. If it did not, describe the possible reasons why your group was different than the model discussed.

1. Stage 1: Preaffiliation/ Approach and avoidance behavior

2. Stage 2: Power and control/A time of transition

3. Stage 3: Intimacy/Developing a familial frame of reference

4. Stage 4: Differentiation/Developing group identity and an internal frame of reference

5. Stage 5: Separation/Breaking away

Goal: To develop comfort in addressing challenging group situations in a phase-appropriate manner.

Focus Competencies or Practice Behaviors:
- EP 2.1.6b Use research evidence to inform practice
- EP 2.1.7a Utilize conceptual frameworks to guide the processes of assessment, intervention, and evaluation
- EP 2.1.9a Continuously discover, appraise, and attend to changing locales, populations, scientific and technological developments, and emerging societal trends to provide relevant services
- EP 2.1.10a Substantively and affectively prepare for action with individuals, families, groups, organizations, and communities
- EP 2.1.10g Select appropriate intervention strategies
- EP 2.1.10i Implement prevention interventions that enhance client capacities
- EP 2.1.10j Help clients resolve problems
- EP 2.1.10l Facilitate transitions and endings

For each of the following challenging situations, identify how you would address the issue and the developmental phase of the group (outlined below). Describe the basis for your decision or any assumptions and group context that affected your choice.

Stages in Group Development
- Stage 1: Preaffiliation
- Stage 2: Power and control
- Stage 3: Intimacy
- Stage 4: Differentiation
- Stage 5: Separation

1. During Stage 2, you find that a member is using a digital recorder to record group meetings

   a. I would say/do:

   b. My actions depend on:

2. During Stage 1 of a psychoeducational group for parents of adults with SPMI, one of the parents falls asleep and snores loudly.

   a. I would say/do:

   b. My actions depend on:

3. During Stage 2 of a parenting group, several of the members challenge your credentials to lead the group as you have never had children.

    a. I would say/do:

    b. My actions depend on:

4. During Stage 4, you learn that members of an anorexia treatment group are participating in social networking sites that promote anorexia and share strategies for disguising weight loss.

    a. I would say/do:

    b. My actions depend on:

5. During Stage 1, members of substance abuse group ask you if you have ever used drugs.

    a. I would say/do:

    b. My actions depend on:

6. During Stage 2 of a residential group for women with addictions, one older adult member says, "I don't belong here with these whores and tramps. All I ever did was take the pills my doctor gave me."

    a. I would say/do:

    b. My actions depend on:

7. During Stage 1 of a bereavement group for children, one member sobs constantly and loudly throughout the session.

    a. I would say/do:

    b. My actions depend on:

Exercise 16.3
Assessing Online Groups

Goal: To critically evaluate the pros and cons of online groups.

Focus Competencies or Practice Behaviors:
- EP 2.1.6b Use research evidence to inform practice
- EP 2.1.7a Utilize conceptual frameworks to guide the processes of assessment, intervention, and evaluation
- EP 2.1.9a Continuously discover, appraise, and attend to changing locales, populations, scientific and technological developments, and emerging societal trends to provide relevant services
- EP 2.1.10a Substantively and affectively prepare for action with individuals, families, groups, organizations, and communities
- EP 2.1.10g Select appropriate intervention strategies
- EP 2.1.10i Implement prevention interventions that enhance client capacities
- EP 2.1.10j Help clients resolve problems
- EP 2.1.10l Facilitate transitions and endings

Go to the website www.supportgroups.com. Select and join a group appropriate to you. There are sites for healthy eating, vegetarians, singles, and other groups, in addition to problem-oriented topics. Alternatively, if you are already in an online support group (Weight Watchers, smoking cessation, etc.) you can use it instead. You should not identify the focus/subject matter of the group you joined. However, you should participate in the group (reading posts, posting if you like) for a minimum of two weeks. Then you should address the following questions. Your instructor may follow up with class discussion about your findings and the pros and cons of online support groups.

1. Assess the quality of the group. Did you find it helpful? Did you find the advice sound?

2. Would you have any apprehensions referring clients to the group you joined? What informed consent would you offer?

3. Did you have any apprehensions participating in the group?

4. Are there any clients you would dissuade from using online groups, based on your experience?

5. What could you determine about the nature of the group membership, in terms of diversity, experience with the topic, integrity, netiquette?

6. Discuss any other features of the group that you observed, including

    a. Cohesion

    b. Rules

    c. Norms

    d. Breadth of participation

    e. Roles

    f. Subgroups

In sum, what do you conclude about the pros and cons of online support groups?

Exercise 16.4
Culturally Competent Group Work

Goal: To seek evidence-based knowledge to enhance cultural competence.

Focus Competencies or Practice Behaviors:
- EP 2.1.6b Use research evidence to inform practice
- EP 2.1.7a Utilize conceptual frameworks to guide the processes of assessment, intervention, and evaluation
- EP 2.1.9a Continuously discover, appraise, and attend to changing locales, populations, scientific and technological developments, and emerging societal trends to provide relevant services
- EP 2.1.10a Substantively and affectively prepare for action with individuals, families, groups, organizations, and communities
- EP 2.1.10g Select appropriate intervention strategies
- EP 2.1.10i Implement prevention interventions that enhance client capacities
- EP 2.1.10j Help clients resolve problems
- EP 2.1.10l Facilitate transitions and endings

Your instructor should divide the class into groups of 5. Your group's task is to research and design a class presentation, with bibliography, on effective groups for diverse populations.

- 189 -

© 2013 Cengage Learning. All Rights Reserved. May not be scanned, copied or duplicated, or posted to a publicly accessible website, in whole or in part.

The presentation can focus on 1) the skills social workers need to be culturally competent group leaders, 2) a review of the best practices in group work for various populations, or 3) a summary of adjustments a group leader might make in assuring that a group on a particular topic (bereavement, parenting, etc.) is culturally appropriate.

Your instructor will inform you about the timeline for the project, the length and format of your presentation, whether it will be demonstrated for the class or just submitted, etc. Otherwise, it is up to your group to make decisions about your topic, roles and responsibilities, workplan, expected outcomes, etc.

When you are finished, address the following questions.

1. How useful and accessible was the research literature on your topic?

2. What can be done to assist busy social workers in utilizing the literature to inform their practices?

3. What are the top three things you learned about culturally competent group work?

4. Does group work with diverse populations differ from family or individual work with the same populations? Comment.

5. What three steps can you take to ensure that once you graduate your practice is up-to-date with new knowledge, social trends and emerging technologies?

Exercise 16.5
Task Group Membership

Goal: To experience and apply the concepts of task group membership in enhancing knowledge of culturally competent group work.

Focus Competencies or Practice Behaviors:
- EP 2.1.6b Use research evidence to inform practice
- EP 2.1.7a Utilize conceptual frameworks to guide the processes of assessment, intervention, and evaluation
- EP 2.1.10a Substantively and affectively prepare for action with individuals, families, groups, organizations, and communities
- EP 2.1.10g Select appropriate intervention strategies

Based on your experience in Exercise 11.4, address the following questions to determine the extent to which your group experience aligned with the concepts associated with task groups.

1. Did your group have a leader? If so, how was that person identified? Was that process satisfactory? Was the leadership effective? If there was no formal leader, please comment on the pros and cons of the process you did use.

2. Describe the group membership. Did members have the skills to carry out the tasks for the group? Would another method of selecting group members have been more effective?

3. Describe the formal and informal roles played by each member of your group.

4. Describe the rules and norms utilized by your group.

5. How often did your group meet? For how long? Where? Were the meetings effective?

6. How were group decisions made? Was this process satisfactory? How would you improve it?

7. How did your group manage conflict?

8. Did subgroups emerge in your group? What effect did they have on the group's work?

9. How closely did your group's behaviors conform to the stages of group development?

10. Would you say your group was successful? By what measure would you evaluate your success?

11. Name one thing you learned about operating effective task groups?

12. Name one thing you learned about group work for diverse populations.

13. Name one thing you learned about yourself as a group member.

Role Play Exercise 16.6
The Five Session Support Group

Goal: To develop experiential knowledge of group work skills and concepts in action.

Focus Competencies or Practice Behaviors:

- EP 2.1.7a Utilize conceptual frameworks to guide the processes of assessment, intervention, and evaluation
- EP 2.1.10a Substantively and affectively prepare for action with individuals, families, groups, organizations, and communities
- EP 2.1.10g Select appropriate intervention strategies
- EP 2.1.10i Implement prevention interventions that enhance client capacities
- EP 2.1.10j Help clients resolve problems
- EP 2.1.10l Facilitate transitions and endings

Your instructor should create groups of 6-7 class members each and select two of those members to serve as group co-facilitators. The purpose of the groups is to "help members be academically successful." The groups will meet for 5 sessions, 30 minutes per session. The sessions can take place during class time or outside of class. The students portraying the group clients should behave as authentically as possible in light of the fact that this is a legitimate group focused on a topic from which most people can benefit. That said, members are not playing themselves in the group but rather members with the following personae. Please select the one you would like to play.

- A member who had poor preparation in his/her previous education and is in danger of flunking out.
- A member who fears he/she was admitted to this program by accident and is highly anxious about the assignments.
- A member who is a single parent returning to school after many years away.
- A member who is the youngest in the class and wonders if he/she knows enough to compete with fellow students.
- A member who has sleep apnea and has difficulty concentrating on readings and staying awake in class.

- A member who has ADHD and has difficulty organizing assignments and workload to meet deadlines.

- A member who has a part-time job, 2 roommates, 3 dogs, and is coach of the ultimate Frisbee team and chair of the campus campaign for peace.

- A member for whom English is a second language and whose family often contacts him/her for assistance with siblings in trouble.

After the group has met for five sessions, describe the group process and leadership skills you observed and identify the strengths and weaknesses you observed in the leaders and the ways your practice as a group leader will be enhanced by this experience.

STAGE   DYNAMICS   LEADER FOCUS

Name: _____ Date: _____

Supervisor's Name: _____

Focus Competencies/Practice Behaviors:

- EP 2.1.6b Use research evidence to inform practice
- EP 2.1.7a Utilize conceptual frameworks to guide the processes of assessment, intervention, and evaluation
- EP 2.1.9a Continuously discover, appraise, and attend to changing locales, populations, scientific and technological developments, and emerging societal trends to provide relevant services
- EP 2.1.10a Substantively and affectively prepare for action with individuals, families, groups, organizations, and communities
- EP 2.1.10g Select appropriate intervention strategies
- EP 2.1.10i Implement prevention interventions that enhance client capacities
- EP 2.1.10j Help clients resolve problems
- EP 2.1.10l Facilitate transitions and endings

Instructions: Evaluate your work or your partner's work in the Focus Practice Behaviors by completing the Practice Behaviors Assessment form below. What other Practice Behaviors did you use to complete these Exercises? Be sure to record them in your assessments.

1.	I have attained this competency/practice behavior (in the range of 80 to 100%)
2.	I have largely attained this competency/practice behavior (in the range of 60 to 80%)
3.	I have partially attained this competency/practice behavior (in the range of 40 to 60%)
4.	I have made a little progress in attaining this competency/practice behavior (in the range of 20 to 40%
5.	I have made almost no progress in attaining this competency/practice behavior (in the range of 0 to 20%)

| EPAS 2008 Core Competencies & Core Practice Behaviors | Student Self Assessment | | | | | | Evaluator Feedback |
Student and Evaluator Assessment Scale and Comments	0	1	2	3	4	5	Agree/Disagree/Comments
2.1.1 Identity as a Professional Social Worker and Conduct Oneself Accordingly:							
a. Advocate for client access to the services of social work							
b. Practice personal reflection and self-correction to assure continual professional development							
c. Attend to professional roles and boundaries							

d. Demonstrate professional demeanor in behavior, appearance, and communication						
e. Engage in career-long learning						
f. Use supervision and consultation						
2.1.2 Apply Social Work Ethical Principles to Guide Professional Practice:						
a. Recognize and manage personal values in a way that allows professional values to guide practice						
b. Make ethical decisions by applying NASW Code of Ethics and, as applicable, IFSW/IASSW Ethics in Social Work, Statement of Principles						
c. Tolerate ambiguity in resolving ethical conflicts						
d. Apply strategies in resolving ethical conflicts						
2.1.3 Apply Critical Thinking to Inform and Communicate Professional Judgments:						
a. Distinguish, appraise, and integrate multiple sources of knowledge, including research-based knowledge and practice wisdom						
b. Analyze models of assessment, prevention, intervention, and evaluation						
c. Demonstrate effective oral and written communication in working with individuals, families, groups, organizations, communities, and colleagues						
2.1.4 Engage Diversity and Difference in Practice:						
a. Recognize the extent to which a culture's structures and values may oppress, marginalize, alienate, or create or enhance privilege and power						
b. Gain sufficient self-awareness to eliminate the influence of personal biases and values in working with diverse groups						
c. Recognize and communicate their understanding of the importance of difference in shaping life experiences						

d. View themselves as learners and engage those with whom they work as informants								
2.1.5 Advance Human Rights and Social and Economic Justice								
a. Understand forms and mechanisms of oppression and discrimination								
b. Advocate for human rights and social and economic justice								
c. Engage in practices that advance social and economic justice								
2.1.6 Engage in research-informed practice and practice-informed research								
a. Use practice experience to inform scientific inquiry								
b. Use research evidence to inform practice								
2.1.7 Apply knowledge of human behavior and the social environment:								
a. Utilize conceptual frameworks to guide the processes of assessment, intervention, and evaluation								
b. Critique and apply knowledge to understand person and environment								
2.1.8 Engage in policy practice to advance social and economic well-being and to deliver effective social work services:								
a. Analyze, formulate, and advocate for policies that advance social well-being								
b. Collaborate with colleagues and clients for effective policy action								
2.1.9 Respond to contexts that shape practice:								
a. Continuously discover, appraise, and attend to changing locales, populations, scientific and technological developments, and emerging societal trends to provide relevant services								
b. Provide leadership in promoting sustainable changes in service delivery and practice to improve the quality of social services								
2.1.10 Engage, assess, intervene, and evaluate with individuals, families, groups, organizations and communities:								
a. Substantively and affectively prepare for action with individuals, families, groups, organizations, and communities								

b. Use empathy and other interpersonal skills							
c. Develop a mutually agreed-on focus of work and desired outcomes							
d. Collect, organize, and interpret client data							
e. Assess client strengths and limitations							
f. Develop mutually agreed-on intervention goals and objectives							
g. Select appropriate intervention strategies.							
h. Initiate actions to achieve organizational goals							
i. Implement prevention interventions that enhance client capacities							
j. Help clients resolve problems							
k. Negotiate, mediate, and advocate for clients							
l. Facilitate transitions and endings							
m. Critically analyze, monitor, and evaluate interventions							

Exercise 17.1
Practicing additive empathy

Goal: to be able to express an empathy response that adds to the client's expression by referring to client thoughts and emotions not directly expressed.

Focus Competencies or Practice Behaviors:
- EP 2.1.10 Engage, assess, intervene and evaluate with individuals families and groups.
- EP 2.1.10b Use empathy and other interpersonal skills

Guidelines for additive empathy and interpretation are presented in your text in Chapter 17. Take each of the following expressions and practice developing an additive empathic response.

1. Client is Cambodian woman who speaks English as a second language. She reports that she is struggling with parenting her stepson, who is 17. She had hoped that he would be looking at going to college but rather is hanging out with friends that she does not approve of. She also reports that communication between them is strained. "My stepson, he does not care about his future, just hanging out with his friends. Everything I try to do, he rejects it."

2. Client is an undocumented woman originally from Mexico. She reports that her ex-husband left her after he started an affair with another woman. Her daughter is unhappy with her and thinks she is responsible for all of the problems they are experiencing. She has limited financial resources and is now living with her sister. She says: "My daughter still loves her father and blames me for breaking up with him. I have been trying hard to keep everything together but I get a little depressed and it is hard to just go on as if nothing has happened. So that's where I'm at now."

3. Rebecca is a college student who reports high stress, feeling overwhelmed and a lack of family support. "I just get so scared and overwhelmed and think I am in here over my head, maybe I am not good enough to do this stuff. I am the first one from my family to go to college and my family members don't really seem to think it is important for me to make it. They would be happy if I would just get a job, meet someone and get married. I have done it before but I am really down this time and don't know if I can pull out of it."

4. Rafael is living with his girlfriend who is supporting him while he is writing a novel. He frets that she won't make enough and he will have to get a job that will prevent him from writing his novel. He has a disability that has not been diagnosed but which might provide him with support if confirmed. "I just think this thing with Jolene may not work out. She won't make enough and I will have to get a regular job and won't be able to write the way I want to. I could do that disability thing but I don't really like to think of myself that way. It feels as if I am between a rock and a hard place."

Exercise 17.2
Practice interpretation

Goal: to explore making tentative explanations for client behavior, thoughts or emotions that have not occurred to the client.

Focus Competencies or Practice Behaviors:
- EP 2.1.10 Engage, assess, intervene and evaluate with individuals families and groups.
- EP 2.1.10b Use empathy and other interpersonal skills

Your text introduced guidelines for interpretation. Take each of the following expressions and practice developing a tentative interpretation.

1. Maurice is about to graduate as an engineer. He wants to leave the state and has sent out many applications. He has also recently come out as a gay man. Some of the areas where he is applying do not have a reputation of being hospitable to openly gay persons. He has been putting off following up on his applications and frets that he will end up living in his parents' basement.

2. Martha wants to set boundaries with her 24-year-old daughter. They are currently living together, but she feels like their relationship is too meshed. Her daughter relies on her for transportation, so they end up doing a lot of activities together. Also, Martha has expressed that sometimes her daughter is more of a friend or counselor than a family member and she recognizes that this is not a healthy mother-daughter relationship. She would like to develop more friendships with people her own age and not feel so lonely and dependent on her daughter.

3. Maria's family are citizens who were originally from Mexico. She got involved with a group of teens who were using drugs and skipping school. Her parents moved her to a new school. She misses her old friends and is very angry at her father, who she says does not listen to her or treat her as a soon-to-be adult. She has been a good student but does not feel very motivated now.

4. Delphine is a 21-year-old woman who dated a man for several years whom she later learned was unfaithful to her. He became increasingly controlling and verbally abusive throughout the course of their relationship. She reports that she has had difficulty trusting her new boyfriend from the beginning of their relationship, which can be attributed to her experiences with her previous partner. She often reads his texts and e-mails to see if he is being faithful to her, and recently discovered an e-mail that he had written to another woman, implying sexual motives. Her boyfriend denied writing this e-mail, but Carolyn does not believe him and is now struggling with whether she should trust him.

Exercise 17.3
Practice appropriate confrontation behavior

Goal: To carry out an appropriate confrontation. .
Focus Competencies or Practice Behaviors:
- EP 2.1.10 Engage, assess, intervene and evaluate with individuals families and groups.
- EP 2.1.10b Use empathy and other interpersonal skills

Guidelines for appropriate confrontation are presented in Chapter 17. With the following situations, practice formulating an appropriate confrontive response.

1. Maria (from #3 of Exercise 17.2, above) has stated that she wants to get back at her father by dropping out of school and getting high with her friends. She wants so much to disappoint him and has given up on wishing that he would treat her like a grown up.

2. Rafael (from #4 from Exercise 17.1, above) has indicated his disappointment with his girlfriend for not being able to support him enough to keep him free to be a writer. He also is avoiding being assessed for a disability which might relieve some of his financial concerns.

3. Ms. Robertson is experiencing high conflict with her adolescent daughter Roberta. She reports that Roberta violates curfew, is often truant and smokes weed with friends. She grounds Roberta and Roberta violates it. Meanwhile Roberta reports that Ms. Robertson does not really know her friends, that they are not all troublemakers. She feels that her mother disrespects her friends. At one time, they enjoyed cooking together.

4. Martin enrolled in a GED program at night but did not attend. He says that he just wants a job, a good job, and is frustrated that his applications have not been accepted.

Exercise 17.4
Put it all together: Role Play practice

Goal: To be able to appropriately carry out additive empathy, interpretations and confrontations in a role play.
Focus Competencies or Practice Behaviors:

- EP 2.1.10a Substantively and affectively prepare for action with individuals, families, groups.
- EP 2.1.10b Use empathy and other interpersonal skills.

This activity works best if there is an observer to the role play. Select one of the following situations or one of your choosing. The observer can monitor your employment of appropriate additive empathy, interpretation or confrontation. The observer for each situation can use the tables below to provide feedback. Carry out the role play for about 10 minutes then give feedback. Note that the role play should occur in the context of a trusting relationship unless there is a circumstance of imminent danger or law violation.

Role Play Exercises: Client 1

You are a part of a county children's crisis response team, You responded to a frantic mother stating that her son was "out of control." Upon arrival the client (Charles, 15) was chasing his mother around the house with a machete. The police were called and John was placed in the county JDC. When you meet with Charles, he says that he does not like living with his mother who is divorced from his father. Charles' family is Hmong and typically when there is a separation, male children go with the father and his clan. In this case, however, Charles could not be controlled by his father so he had to move. Charles says he has no friends in the new school, that his mother and he have different religions: she is a Christian and he is an Animist. He wants to be respected and not pestered all the time. As your contact with this client is early and a relationship is not yet established, you might be able to explore a potential discrepancy but not effectively carry out an interpretation or confrontation.

Role Play Exercises: Client 2

Your 15-year-old client Marsha is doing very well academically in school but has had considerable conflict with her family because she is dating an older male who has dropped out of school and who is ethnically different from her. She has just shared with you that she has figured out the solution to her situation. She will get pregnant by Rory, her boyfriend, and then she will move out and raise this child on her own or with Rory. She knows that she could be a better parent than either one she has had. Assume that you have now seen Marsha for several months. She has not gotten pregnant and has concluded that Rory would not be a responsible parent. She wants to go to college but still does not see how she can continue to live with her parents and be supported by them.

Role Play Exercises: Client 3

Floyd has emphysema and recently met with his doctor. The doctor has recommended that he stop smoking. Floyd reports " So the doctor says I won't last long unless I quit smoking. But I have been smoking since I was 14 years old. I have tried to stop lots of times but it never lasted." Now assume that Floyd has returned for a follow-up visit and he reports that he has reduced his smoking but been unable to stop completely.

Role Play Exercises: Client 4

Esmirelda has been gang involved but is now placed in a foster placement far from her home and the gang she was part of. She is attending school now and doing well. She has decided that she might want to become a probation officer or a social worker. She however considers members of her gang to be her family. Esmirelda meets with you for weekly sessions.

Role Play Exercises: Assessment Tables

Assessment of Additive Empathy or Interpretation Usage		
	yes	*no*
1. Utilized when sound relationship has evolved		

		yes	no
2.	Utilized when client is engaged in self-exploration or have shown selves to be ready to do so		
3.	Avoids making several interpretations in succession		
4.	Phrases interpretations tentatively		
5.	Notes reactions to interpretation		
6.	Acknowledges possible error if client disagrees with interpretation		

Assessment of Appropriate Confrontation		
	yes	*no*
1. Employed with law violation or situation of imminent danger		

2. Conveyed in manner conveying
    a. Your concern in an "I" statement
    b. Relates to client goal
    c. Presents discrepant behaviour, thought, emotion or action
    d. Describes probable consequences		

3. Avoided until working relationship established		
4. Use sparingly		
5. Convey warmth, caring and concern		
6. Encourages self-confrontation		
7. Avoids when client is under significant strain		
8. Follows confrontation with empathic responsiveness		
9. Expects client to respond with some anxiety		
10. Does not expect immediate change		

Chapter 17
Competencies/Practice Behaviors Exercises Assessment:

Name: _____ Date: _____

Supervisor's Name: _____

Focus Competencies and Practice Behaviors:
- EP 2.1.10a Substantively and affectively prepare for action with individuals, families, groups.
- EP 2.1.10b Use empathy and other interpersonal skills

Instructions: Evaluate your work or your partner's work in the Focus Practice Behaviors by completing the Practice Behaviors Assessment form below. What other Practice Behaviors did you use to complete these Exercises? Be sure to record them in your assessments. Please note that as you are beginning your work in this course, high level attainment of competencies at this point in your program is not anticipated. Over the course of this course and this program, your proficiency should increase to the point that you and other competent assessors will agree that you have attained the competency at a satisfactory level.

1.	I have attained this competency/practice behavior (in the range of 80 to 100%)
2.	I have largely attained this competency/practice behavior (in the range of 60 to 80%)
3.	I have partially attained this competency/practice behavior (in the range of 40 to 60%)
4.	I have made a little progress in attaining this competency/practice behavior (in the range of 20 to 40%
5.	I have made almost no progress in attaining this competency/practice behavior (in the range of 0 to 20%)

EPAS 2008 Core Competencies & Core Practice Behaviors	Student Self Assessment						Evaluator Feedback
Student and Evaluator Assessment Scale and Comments	0	1	2	3	4	5	Agree/Disagree/Comments
2.1.1 Identity as a Professional Social Worker and Conduct Oneself Accordingly:							
a. Advocate for client access to the services of social work							
b. Practice personal reflection and self-correction to assure continual professional development							
c. Attend to professional roles and boundaries							
d. Demonstrate professional demeanor in behavior, appearance, and communication							
e. Engage in career-long learning							
f. Use supervision and consultation							

2.1.2 Apply Social Work Ethical Principles to Guide Professional Practice:								
a. Recognize and manage personal values in a way that allows professional values to guide practice								
b. Make ethical decisions by applying NASW Code of Ethics and, as applicable, IFSW/IASSW Ethics in Social Work, Statement of Principles								
c. Tolerate ambiguity in resolving ethical conflicts								
d. Apply strategies in resolving ethical conflicts								
2.1.3 Apply Critical Thinking to Inform and Communicate Professional Judgments:								
a. Distinguish, appraise, and integrate multiple sources of knowledge, including research-based knowledge and practice wisdom								
b. Analyze models of assessment, prevention, intervention, and evaluation								
c. Demonstrate effective oral and written communication in working with individuals, families, groups, organizations, communities, and colleagues								
2.1.4 Engage Diversity and Difference in Practice:								
a. Recognize the extent to which a culture's structures and values may oppress, marginalize, alienate, or create or enhance privilege and power								
b. Gain sufficient self-awareness to eliminate the influence of personal biases and values in working with diverse groups								
c. Recognize and communicate their understanding of the importance of difference in shaping life experiences								
d. View themselves as learners and engage those with whom they work as informants								
2.1.5 Advance Human Rights and Social and Economic Justice								
a. Understand forms and mechanisms of oppression and discrimination								

b. Advocate for human rights and social and economic justice							
c. Engage in practices that advance social and economic justice							
2.1.6 Engage in research-informed practice and practice-informed research							
a. Use practice experience to inform scientific inquiry							
b. Use research evidence to inform practice							
2.1.7 Apply knowledge of human behavior and the social environment:							
a. Utilize conceptual frameworks to guide the processes of assessment, intervention, and evaluation							
b. Critique and apply knowledge to understand person and environment							
2.1.8 Engage in policy practice to advance social and economic well-being and to deliver effective social work services:							
a. Analyze, formulate, and advocate for policies that advance social well-being							
b. Collaborate with colleagues and clients for effective policy action							
2.1.9 Respond to contexts that shape practice:							
a. Continuously discover, appraise, and attend to changing locales, populations, scientific and technological developments, and emerging societal trends to provide relevant services							
b. Provide leadership in promoting sustainable changes in service delivery and practice to improve the quality of social services							
2.1.10 Engage, assess, intervene, and evaluate with individuals, families, groups, organizations and communities:							
a. Substantively and affectively prepare for action with individuals, families, groups, organizations, and communities							
b. Use empathy and other interpersonal skills							
c. Develop a mutually agreed-on focus of work and desired outcomes							
d. Collect, organize, and interpret client data							
e. Assess client strengths and limitations							

f. Develop mutually agreed-on intervention goals and objectives							
g. Select appropriate intervention strategies.							
h. Initiate actions to achieve organizational goals							
i. Implement prevention interventions that enhance client capacities							
j. Help clients resolve problems							
k. Negotiate, mediate, and advocate for clients							
l. Facilitate transitions and endings							
m. Critically analyze, monitor, and evaluate interventions							

Chapter 18	
Managing Barriers to Change	

Exercise 18.1	
How Would You React?	

Goal: To develop insight into reactions, emotions, feelings, and conflicts, that can arise in social work practice.

Focus Competencies and Practice Behaviors
- EP 2.1.1b Practice personal reflection and self-correction to assure continual professional development
- EP 2.1.1c Attend to professional roles and boundaries
- EP 2.1.1d Demonstrate professional demeanor in behavior, appearances, and communications
- EP 2.1.1f Use supervision and consultation
- EP 2.1.2a Recognize and manage personal values in a way that allows for professional values to guide practice
- EP 2.1.10a Substantively and effectively prepare for action with individuals, families, groups, organizations, and communities

Rate each of the following vignettes on the 1-5 scale below to reflect your reaction to the situation:

1. Strong negative reaction
2. Moderate negative reaction
3. Neutral Reaction
4. Strong positive reaction
5. Moderate positive reaction

Then identify the beliefs, emotions or feelings associated with your reaction and the effects that your reaction could have on your ability to work with the individual involved.

Describe the steps that you would take to address your reactions and uphold your professional responsibility.

At the conclusion of the exercise:
1. Discuss and rate what you learned about yourself.
2. Identify clients or situations that you recognize as posing difficulties for you and your anticipated reactions and uphold your professional responsibilities.

How Would You React: Vignette A

You are a social work student intern in a family service agency. You are meeting with a college aged females who recently learned that she was pregnant. Her boyfriend had left the city, and he warned her not to tell his parents about the pregnancy. Currently she is homeless because her parents demanded that she leave their home because of their shame about her out-of-wedlock pregnancy.

1   2   3   4   5

Identify the beliefs, emotions and feelings associated with your reaction.

Describe the effects that your beliefs, reactions or feelings in this situation could have as you continue to work with this client.

Describe the steps that you would take to address your reactions and uphold your professional responsibility.

How Would You React: Vignette B

A 16-year -old male client became angry with you because you refused to give him a bus card. You explained to him that resources are limited, and further, this is his second request for a bus card in less than two weeks. In response, he stated "That ain't your business. Your job is to help me!"

1   2   3   4   5

Identify the beliefs, emotions or feelings associated with your reaction.

Describe the effects that your reaction could have on your ability to continue working with this client.

Describe the steps that you would take to address your reactions and uphold your professional responsibility.

How Would You React: Vignette C

Your client often shows up late for appointment with you and when she arrives, she is generally disagreeable, disorganized and demanding. In this particular session, she tells you that she had not taken the time to complete the tasks that she had previously agreed to, so that she could regain custody of her four children.

1	2	3	4	5

Identify the beliefs, emotions or feelings associated with your reaction.

Describe the effects that your reaction could have on your ability to continue working with this client.

Describe the steps that you would take to address your reactions and uphold your professional responsibility.

How Would You React: Vignette D

The youth that you are working with is doing well. He is completing his senior year in high school, despite the fact that his home life is often chaotic and unstable. He is hoping to go to college. Recently, the school' security officer found him smoking marijuana behind a school building. The incident was reported to you because he has been suspended from school. This is your first meeting with him after his suspension.

1	2	3	4	5

Identify the beliefs, emotions or feelings associated with your reaction.

Describe the effects that your reaction could have on your ability to continue working with this client.

Describe the steps that you would take to address your reactions and uphold your professional responsibility.

How Would You React: Vignette E

You are meeting with a mother and her daughter, age 15 years. Throughout the session, the mother continually points out the daughter's faults, attributing them to her father's family. The mother speaks in a whiney voice, and she presents herself as "poor me." In response, the daughter describes her mother as uncaring. She emphasizes that her mother refuses to let her allow her friends to come to the house. Furthermore, this is the reason that she hangs out with her friends on a nearby street corner. Hearing this, the mother explodes, stating, "I'm not about to let you be friends with those people, they are drug dealers, gang members and I don't know what else they are up to." The daughter responds, "You don't know what you are talking about. At least I'm not pregnant like you, at my age!"

1   2   3   4   5

Identify the beliefs, emotions or feelings associated with your reaction.

Describe the effects that your reaction could have on your ability to continue working with the mother and daughter.

Describe the steps that you would take to address your reactions and uphold your professional responsibility.

How Would You React: Vignette G

At the conclusion of a session, an adult client stands in front of asked you to give him or her, a hug, because he or she is feeling sad.

1   2   3   4   5

Identify the beliefs, emotions or feelings associated with your reaction.

Describe the effects that your reaction could have on your ability to continue working with this client.

Describe the steps that you would take to address your reactions and uphold your professional responsibility.

How Would You React: Vignette H

You are working with a school-based social skills group. During a group session, one of the group members stated. "People like you don't like kids like me. You are only doing this group because you get paid to be here." Some of the members in the group laugh.

1   2   3   4   5

Identify the beliefs, emotions or feelings associated with your reaction.

Describe the effects that your reaction could have on your ability to continue working with this member of the group.

Describe the steps that you would take to address your reactions and uphold your professional responsibility.

How Would You React: Vignette I

You have been working with an elderly male. He expresses very strong opinions about gender roles and persons of color, especially foreign-born individuals who he believes are taking jobs from honest, hard-working American citizens. According to him, everyone, including women, should stay in their place, like it was in his day.

1   2   3   4   5

Identify the beliefs, emotions or feelings associated with your reaction.

Describe the effects that your reaction could have on your ability to continue working with this client.

Describe the steps that you would take to address your reactions and uphold your professional responsibility.

How Would You React: Summary

Describe and rate your level of learning about yourself as a result of completing this exercise.

Rating Scale:

1	2	3	4	5
Low		Moderate		High

Identify clients, problems or situations that you recognize as posing difficulties for you and your anticipated reactions.

Discuss the steps that you would take in resolving the identified difficulties and uphold your professional responsibilities.

© 2013 Cengage Learning. All Rights Reserved. May not be scanned, copied or duplicated, or posted to a publicly accessible website, in whole or in part.

Goal: To assist you in implementing strategies that facilitates clients' capacities to change.

Focus Competencies and Practice Behaviors
- EP 2.1.7a Utilize conceptual frameworks to guide the process of assessment, intervention, and evaluation
- EP 2.1.10a Substantively and effectively prepare for action with individuals, families, groups, organizations and communities
- EP 2.1.10b Use empathy and other interpersonal skills
- EP 2.1.10i Implement preventions that enhance client capacities
- EP 2.1.10j Help clients resolve problems

To complete the exercise review the content and the table in Chapter 17 on *Stages of Change.* Then view the video, "How Can I Help?" featuring Peter as the social worker who is working with Julie, the client.

Focus your observations on Peter's behavior, and the influence that his behavior had on Julie's motivation. Following the prompts, answer the following questions.

1. Identify the issue or issues in which Julie appeared to be in the Contemplation Stage of Change, but has yet to take action.

2. Discuss the guiding principles of Motivational Interviewing the Peter used to encourage Julie to take action.

3. In the *spirit* of Motivational Interviewing, describe how Peter's work with Julie was guided by the following:

   a. Collaborating with Julie:

   b. Drawing out Julie's intrinsic motivation (Evocation):

   c. Reinforcing and respecting Julie's self-determination and autonomy:

   d. Describe issue in which Julie seemed to be in the Precontemplation Stage of Change.

- 215 -

4. Describe the techniques and principles that Peter used in assisting Julie to consider moving beyond this stage.

5. Describe how Julie responded.

6. Identify any particular time (or times) during the session that may have caused you to react, decide to take charge, and use a different approach with Julie. Indicate the basis for your decision.

<table>
<tr><td style="text-align:center">Exercise 18.2
Motivating Change Role-Play</td></tr>
</table>

Goal: To assist you in gaining an understanding the potential reactions of clients.

Focus Competencies and Practice Behaviors
- EP 2.1.7a Utilize conceptual frameworks to guide the process of assessment, intervention, and evaluation
- EP 2.1.10a Substantively and effectively prepare for action with individuals, families, groups, organizations and communities
- EP 2.1.10b Use empathy and other interpersonal skills
- EP 2.1.10i Implement preventions that enhance client capacities
- EP 2.1.10j Help clients resolve problems

Identify a behavior or situation in which you have considered changing. Determine which of the change stages that best represent your thinking. Then unvite a classmate to role-play in which you are the client, and the classmate is the social worker. Following the prompts complete the task indicated, and answer the questions that follow.

Client: Open the interview with the social worker by describing the behavior or situation that you want to change, but have yet to take action.

Social Worker: Describe what you would say to the client in confronting his or her inaction, in which you also question his or her motivation to change.

Client: Describe your reaction, emotions and feelings as a result of the social worker's confrontation.

Social Worker and Client: Switch the focus of the session in which you follow the "spirit" and the guiding principles of Motivational Interviewing, in helping the client to change.

1. Social Worker and client: Together, create dialogue in which you describe how you would:

    a. Form a collaborative partnership:

    b. Draw out the client's intrinsic motivation (Evocation):

    c. Encourage autonomy and self-direction:

    d. Emphasize a discrepancy:

    e. Respond to resistance:

    f. Use empathy and other interpersonal skills:

2. Describe the aspects of Motivational Interviewing as a method to motivate change that were clarified for you in completing this exercise.

Exercise 18.3
Learning from a Colleague's Behavior

Goal: To assist you in recognizing behaviors that can indicate over- or- under involvement with clients.

Focused Competencies and Practice Behaviors
- EP 2.1.1c Attend to professional roles and boundaries
- EP 2.1.1d Demonstrate professional demeanor in behavior, appearance and communication

Review the case examples in the chapter in which the social worker was over- or under-involved. The social worker presenting the case and Marta, the youth worker, are your colleagues.

Following the prompts, indicate what you would do.

Case Example 1: Advice for Social Worker presenting a case:

Identify the social worker's specific behaviors, actions or other dynamics that are present in the case.

Discuss how the social worker's behaviors, actions or other dynamics represent relational dynamics that are barriers.

Describe how you would approach the social worker about your concerns.

Describe the profess advice you would offer, and indicate the basis for your decision.

Case Example 2: Advice for Marta, the youth worker in homeless shelter

Identify Marta's specific behaviors, actions or other dynamics that are present in the case.

Discuss how Marta's behaviors, actions or other dynamics represent relational dynamics that are barriers.

Describe how you would approach Marta about your concerns.

Describe the profess advice you would offer, and indicate the basis for your decision.

Exercise 18.5
Developing Cross-Racial, Cross Cultural Relationships

Goal: To assist you in increasing your skills in working with diverse clients

Focus Competencies and Practice Behaviors
- EP 2.1.1b Practice personal reflection and self-correction to assure continued professional development.
- EP 2.1.4d View themselves as learners and engage those with whom they work as key informants
- EP 2.1.7b Critique and apply knowledge to understand the person and environment
- EP 2.1.10a Substantively and effectively prepare for action with individuals, families, groups, organizations and communities

Read the scenario below and then, following the prompts, complete the tasks indicated.

You are meeting with a diverse client in an initial session. You are anxious because you are not entirely familiar with the client's racial or cultural group. The referral summary described the client as difficult. As the session began, you observed that the client appears to be equally uncomfortable.

1. Prior to the initial session, describe the steps that you would take in preparation for meeting with the client.

2. Describe how the preparatory steps would help you in developing a relationship with the client.

3. Discuss the potential relational dynamics that could pose barrier in your developing a relationship with the client and the client with you.

4. Describe how you would demonstrate *cultural empathy* or *relational empathy* as you begin working with the client.

5. Describe specific aspects of "helper attractiveness" that you have that would facilitate your work with the client.

Name: _____ **Date:** _____

Supervisor's Name: _____

Focus Competencies/Practice Behaviors:

- EPAS 2.1.1b Practice personal reflection and self-correction to assure continual growth and professional development
- EPAS 2.1.1c Attend to professional roles and boundaries
- EPAS 2.1.1f Use supervision and consultation
- EPAS 2.1.2a Recognize and manage personal values in a way that allows for professional values to guide practice
- EPAS 2.1.4b Gain sufficient self-awareness to eliminate the influence of personal bias and values in working with diverse groups
- EPAS 2.1.4d View themselves as learners and engage those with whom they work as key informants
- EPAS 2.1.7a Utilize conceptual frameworks to guide the process of assessment, intervention, and evaluation
- EPAS 2.1.7b Critique and apply knowledge to understand person and environment
- EPAS 2.1.10a Substantively and affectively prepare for action with individuals, families, groups, organizations, and communities
- EPAS 2.1.10b Use empathy and other interpersonal skills
- EPAS 2.1.10i Implement prevention interventions that enhance client capacities
- EPAS 2.1.10j Help clients resolve problems

Instructions: Evaluate your work or your partner's work in the Focus Practice Behaviors by completing the Practice Behaviors Assessment form below. What other Practice Behaviors did you use to complete these Exercises? Be sure to record them in your assessments.

1.	I have attained this competency/practice behavior (in the range of 80 to 100%)
2.	I have largely attained this competency/practice behavior (in the range of 60 to 80%)
3.	I have partially attained this competency/practice behavior (in the range of 40 to 60%)
4.	I have made a little progress in attaining this competency/practice behavior (in the range of 20 to 40%
5.	I have made almost no progress in attaining this competency/practice behavior (in the range of 0 to 20%)

EPAS 2008 Core Competencies & Core Practice Behaviors	Student Self Assessment						Evaluator Feedback
Student and Evaluator Assessment Scale and Comments	0	1	2	3	4	5	Agree/Disagree/Comments
2.1.1 Identity as a Professional Social Worker and Conduct Oneself Accordingly:							
a. Advocate for client access to the services of social work							
b. Practice personal reflection and self-correction to assure continual professional development							
c. Attend to professional roles and boundaries							
d. Demonstrate professional demeanor in behavior, appearance, and communication							
e. Engage in career-long learning							
f. Use supervision and consultation							
2.1.2 Apply Social Work Ethical Principles to Guide Professional Practice:							
a. Recognize and manage personal values in a way that allows professional values to guide practice							
b. Make ethical decisions by applying NASW Code of Ethics and, as applicable, IFSW/IASSW Ethics in Social Work, Statement of Principles							
c. Tolerate ambiguity in resolving ethical conflicts							
d. Apply strategies in resolving ethical conflicts							
2.1.3 Apply Critical Thinking to Inform and Communicate Professional Judgments:							
a. Distinguish, appraise, and integrate multiple sources of knowledge, including research-based knowledge and practice wisdom							
b. Analyze models of assessment, prevention, intervention, and evaluation							
c. Demonstrate effective oral and written communication in working with individuals, families, groups, organizations, communities, and colleagues							

2.1.4 Engage Diversity and Difference in Practice:							
a. Recognize the extent to which a culture's structures and values may oppress, marginalize, alienate, or create or enhance privilege and power							
b. Gain sufficient self-awareness to eliminate the influence of personal biases and values in working with diverse groups							
c. Recognize and communicate their understanding of the importance of difference in shaping life experiences							
d. View themselves as learners and engage those with whom they work as informants							
2.1.5 Advance Human Rights and Social and Economic Justice							
a. Understand forms and mechanisms of oppression and discrimination							
b. Advocate for human rights and social and economic justice							
c. Engage in practices that advance social and economic justice							
2.1.6 Engage in research-informed practice and practice-informed research							
a. Use practice experience to inform scientific inquiry							
b. Use research evidence to inform practice							
2.1.7 Apply knowledge of human behavior and the social environment:							
a. Utilize conceptual frameworks to guide the processes of assessment, intervention, and evaluation							
b. Critique and apply knowledge to understand person and environment							
2.1.8 Engage in policy practice to advance social and economic well-being and to deliver effective social work services:							
a. Analyze, formulate, and advocate for policies that advance social well-being							
b. Collaborate with colleagues and clients for effective policy action							

2.1.9 Respond to contexts that shape practice:							
a. Continuously discover, appraise, and attend to changing locales, populations, scientific and technological developments, and emerging societal trends to provide relevant services							
b. Provide leadership in promoting sustainable changes in service delivery and practice to improve the quality of social services							
2.1.10 Engage, assess, intervene, and evaluate with individuals, families, groups, organizations and communities:							
a. Substantively and affectively prepare for action with individuals, families, groups, organizations, and communities							
b. Use empathy and other interpersonal skills							
c. Develop a mutually agreed-on focus of work and desired outcomes							
d. Collect, organize, and interpret client data							
e. Assess client strengths and limitations							
f. Develop mutually agreed-on intervention goals and objectives							
g. Select appropriate intervention strategies.							
h. Initiate actions to achieve organizational goals							
i. Implement prevention interventions that enhance client capacities							
j. Help clients resolve problems							
k. Negotiate, mediate, and advocate for clients							
l. Facilitate transitions and endings							
m. Critically analyze, monitor, and evaluate interventions							

Exercise 19.1
My Comfort with Feedback

Goal: To develop insight into personal reactions to evaluative feedback.

Focus Competencies or Practice Behaviors:
- EP 2.1.1b Practice personal reflection and self-correction to assure continual professional development
- EP 2.1.1f Use supervision and consultation
- EP 2.1.10m Critically analyze, monitor, and evaluate interventions

In the first column, list at least 10 specific situations in which you or your work has been evaluated (on the job, papers or exams, in supervision, etc. In the second column identify the emotions that you experienced before receiving the feedback or evaluation (anxiety, eagerness, tension, fear, etc.). Complete the reflection questions at the end.

The Evaluation	Your Reaction

Reflection Questions

1. As you review the list, what patterns do you notice in your reactions to feedback and evaluation? Does it make a difference who is evaluating you? How positive you expect the review to be? How confident you were in your work?

2. How do you tend to react when faced with critical feedback?

3. Do your supervisors or instructors view you as being open to feedback?

4. How might your reactions to evaluation affect your conversations with clients about case outcomes, processes, and satisfaction with service?

5. What steps can you take to make sure that practice evaluations are not negatively affected by your reactions to feedback?

6. How can data from evaluation be used to improve your practice and the services of your agency?

Exercise 19.2
Evaluating Practice

Goal: To develop strategies for evaluating client satisfaction and social work processes and outcomes.

Focus Competencies or Practice Behaviors:
- EP 2.1.10m Critically analyze, monitor, and evaluate interventions
- EP 2.1.3a Distinguish, appraise, and integrate multiple sources of knowledge, including research-based knowledge and practice wisdom
- EP 2.1.4d View yourself as a learner and engage those with whom you work as informants

Review the case of the case of Josephine (an older adult client depicted in videos accompanying the text and in a biopsychosocial assessment in Chapter 9). Based on your readings about evaluation, describe specific strategies that the worker in that case can use to assess:
- Case Outcomes
- Process
- Client Satisfaction

What measures would you use? What questions would you ask?

1. Methods for Evaluating Outcomes

2. Methods for Evaluating Process

3. Methods for Evaluating Satisfaction

	Exercise 19.3
	Ethics and Endings

Goal: To identify the ethical dimensions in dilemmas occurring during the final phase of the helping process.

Focus Competencies or Practice Behaviors:
- EP 2.1.1b Practice personal reflection and self-correction to assure continual professional development
- EP 2.1.2b Make ethical decisions by applying standards of the National Association of Social Workers Code of Ethics and, as applicable, the International Federation of Social Workers/International Association of Schools of Social Work Ethics in Social Work, Statement of Principles
- EP 2.1.3a Distinguish, appraise, and integrate multiple sources of knowledge, including research-based knowledge and practice wisdom
- EP 2.1.10l Facilitate transitions and endings
- EP 2.1.10m Critically analyze, monitor, and evaluate interventions

The instructor should divide the class members into pairs or groups. Students should review the guidance in Chapter 4 on ethical dilemmas and on ethical decision making. For each of the dilemmas below, class members should discuss how they would respond if they were the workers in the case, the rationale for their responses, and the resources (supervision, consultation, research) they might turn to for assistance.

As a whole class, the following can be used as debriefing questions:
1. Which dilemmas did you find the most difficult? Least? What accounts for those differences?
2. Did students find differences in their responses to dilemmas?
3. In discussing the cases with others, dis students discover new ideas or strategies?
4. Did any responses raise concerns because they did not fit with the NASW Code or other standards?

Students can also be asked to work on their responses individually before discussing them with classmates.

Ethical Dilemma 1

A teen client who is aging out of foster care asks the social worker who has been his guardian to stay in touch with him via Facebook.

Ethical Dilemma 2

During the evaluation process a client states, "There were some things I didn't like here [at the agency] but I'm not going to say because I don't want to get you or me into trouble."

Ethical Dilemma 3

In the final family session the father thanks the social worker and gives him/her a $25 gift certificate to a local restaurant.

Ethical Dilemma 4

The social worker has resigned from the agency, as she is expecting a child. During the final session a client gives her a baby blanket that she has crocheted.

Ethical Dilemma 5

During termination from service at an agency the client asks if he/she can continue to see the worker for care through the social worker's private practice.

Ethical Dilemma 6

An adult male client is dying of AIDS. He asks the hospital social worker to tell his family, after he passes away, that he died of pneumonia.

Ethical Dilemma 7

During the evaluation process, a client gives very negative feedback, indicating he/she was unhappy with services and felt they didn't help much. The supervisor of the worker on the case instructed her to record the feedback as "not received" as including it would "unfairly drag down our scores."

Ethical Dilemma 8

During the evaluation process, a client gives the services and outcomes uniformly outstanding scores. The worker is glad for the good ratings, but is concerned that the client is not being honest in order to avoid discomfort on his part or the workers.

Ethical Dilemma 9

Sharon and her family are leaving a battered women's shelter to move into their own apartment. One of the caseworkers has been cleaning out her house for a yard sale and would like to give Sharon furniture and household goods to help her make a new start.

Exercise 19.4
Strategies for Maintaining Gains

Goal: To understand common barriers to successful maintenance of change and identify strategies to bolster success.

Focus Competencies or Practice Behaviors:
- EP 2.1.3a Distinguish, appraise, and integrate multiple sources of knowledge, including research-based knowledge and practice wisdom.
- EP 2.1.3b Analyze models of assessment, prevention, intervention, and evaluation

Consider a time in your life when you have tried to change (lose weight, stop a bad habit, learn a new skill or sport). Once you made progress to your goal what kinds of things got in the way of maintaining or improving your gains? List at least three of those in the left hand column below. In the right hand column, for each barrier, identify strategies that you could have used to continue change and avoid "relapse." If you have difficulty coming up with ideas, review your text or the literature for strategies for maintaining change. Last, address the question that follows the lists.

Barriers to Continued Change	Ideas for Overcoming Barriers

Reflection question: Based on your insights about the challenges and strategies of maintaining change, what can you do as a social work to help your clients achieve continued success with their goals?

Goal: To develop appropriate, ethical responses to common client reactions to termination.

Focus Competencies or Practice Behaviors:
- EP 2.1.2b Make ethical decisions by applying standards of the National Association of Social Workers Code of Ethics and, as applicable, the International Federation of Social Workers/International Association of Schools of Social Work Ethics in Social Work, Statement of Principles
- EP 2.1.10b Use empathy and other interpersonal skills
- EP 2.1.10l Facilitate transitions and endings
- EP 2.1.3a Distinguish, appraise, and integrate multiple sources of knowledge, including research-based knowledge and practice wisdom

For each client statement below, indicate what your verbatim response would be, then identify the rationale for your response. What feelings and motivations do you detect behind the client's statement? What are you trying to accomplish by your response? How would the context of the case make a difference (characteristics of the client, type of termination, etc.). How does your knowledge of termination reactions come into play in your response?

Client #1: Let's just end now. I don't need to come back for a final session next week.

Social Worker response:

Rationale for response:

Client #2: You never really cared about me anyway. This is just a job for you so it's no problem to move on to the next client.

Social Worker response:

Rationale for response:

Client #3: All you people running this program are so stupid. I just told you I was doing better, but I wasn't.

Social Worker response:

Rationale for response:

Client #4 [family]: Why do we have to end? We were just getting better.

Social Worker response:

Rationale for response:

Client #5: I'm really scared I'm going to start bingeing again. With my new job and other changes in the next few weeks, I think it's a bad time to stop seeing you.

Social Worker response:

Rationale for response:

Client #6: I know the group is over, but can we at least all stay in touch on Facebook?

Social Worker response:

Rationale for response:

Role Play Exercise 19.6
Managing Difficult Endings

Goal: To practice communication strategies for achieving the goals of termination in difficult case situations.

Focus Competencies or Practice Behaviors:
- EP 2.1.1b Practice personal reflection and self-correction to assure continual professional development
- EP 2.1.1f Use supervision and consultation
- EP 2.1.10b Use empathy and other interpersonal skills
- EP 2.1.10l Facilitate transitions and endings
- EP 2.1.4d View yourself as a learner and engage those with whom you work as informants

Review the four key tasks of termination:
1. Evaluating the service provided and the extent to which goals were accomplished
2. Determining when to implement termination
3. Mutually resolving emotional reactions experienced during the process of ending
4. Planning to maintain gains achieved and to achieve continued growth.

Working in pairs chose one of the cases below with one student portraying the client and the other, the social worker. (Some vignettes are suitable for multiple students as they portray family or group terminations). Within the demographics provided, the vignettes can be used flexibly to depict clients and workers of various backgrounds, ages, sexual orientations, etc. and role players are free to improvise facts of the case beyond the information provided in the vignettes.

Alternatively, the role plays can be done in fish-bowl fashion with one group role playing and the rest of the class observing.

At the conclusion of the role plays, the instructor can use the following questions as a guide for debriefing the experience.

1. What features of the case made the termination conversation complex?
2. What emotions did the case evoke in the role players and in the observers? How did those affect communications about termination?
3. What strengths were displayed by the students playing the social workers?
4. What suggestions can be offered to the student social worker for improving skills in the case?

Vignette 1

Carla is a 17-year-old who is in hospice care due to end-stage cancer. Diane/David was her school social worker throughout her illness, acting as a liaison with the teachers on missed assignments and as a support when Carla encountered difficulties returning to school, dealing with peers, and coming to terms with her illness. Carla is lucid but very fatigued. This meeting will be the social worker's last with her.

Vignette 2

Larry is a 22-year-old who was mandated to attend a treatment group* for batterers after he cut his girlfriend in the face and arms during an argument. One criterion for group membership is that clients must refrain from further abusive behavior. Last week Larry kicked in the door of his girlfriend's apartment, demanding to see their daughter, so today will be his final session with the group.

*This vignette can also be played as an individual client-social worker case.

Vignette 3

The XYZ agency lost a grant to provide parenting support and clients receiving services through that program will be terminated in three weeks. Today the social worker is meeting with a client (Shante/Samuel) whom he/she has worked with for several months and must notify her/him of the program closure. No comparable resources are available for referrals.

Vignette 4

The Davis family has attended monthly educational and family sessions during their daughter Dawn's year-long placement for treatment of anorexia. This will be the last session before the final "commencement ceremony" marking the end of Dawn's treatment. The parents are extremely apprehensive about having Dawn return home. They wonder if she is really better and they offer to pay for her to stay longer. Her siblings have mixed feelings about their sister: anger at the attention and expense she has caused, worry for her health, discomfort at having her rejoin the family, and hope that things will now return to normal. Dawn will be at this session with the family. Alternately, this vignette can be done individually with Dawn herself expressing apprehension about her upcoming discharge from the program.

Vignette 5

Ellen/Elden began seeing the social worker 2 months ago after she/he was warned of eviction due to the condition of her/his apartment and the accumulation shopping bags, food containers, magazines and other belongings. Initially, Ellen/Elden enthusiastically participated in sessions, agreeing to tasks and following through on them. Over the last four sessions, however, that motivation has waned. The social worker has shared the observation with her/him and Ellen/Elden has said "I'm trying, but it is just too hard to part with so much useful stuff." The social worker has decided that he/she is no longer being helpful to the client and that he/she must terminate the case.

Vignette 6

Clara is a social worker who has decided to resign following a significant health crisis that is likely to be terminal. She must notify her clients and has talked with her supervisor about how to do so without engaging in excessive self-disclosure or turning the focus on herself instead of the client. Today she is meeting with Ed/Ellen, a longtime client who trusts and relies on Clara. Ed/Ellen has no family, very few social supports, and frequently lives on the street. He/she has expressed fears of abandonment in the past.

Name: _____   **Date:** _____

Supervisor's Name: _____

Focus Competencies/Practice Behaviors:

- EP 2.1.1b Practice personal reflection and self-correction to assure continual professional development
- EP 2.1.1f Use supervision and consultation
- EP 2.1.2b Make ethical decisions by applying standards of the National Association of Social Workers Code of Ethics and, as applicable, the International Federation of Social Workers/International Association of Schools of Social Work Ethics in Social Work, Statement of Principles
- EP 2.1.3a Distinguish, appraise, and integrate multiple sources of knowledge, including research-based knowledge and practice wisdom
- EP 2.1.3b Analyze models of assessment, prevention, intervention, and evaluation
- EP 2.1.4d View yourself as a learner and engage those with whom you work as informants
- EP 2.1.10b Use empathy and other interpersonal skills
- EP 2.1.10l Facilitate transitions and endings
- EP 2.1.10m Critically analyze, monitor, and evaluate interventions

Instructions: Evaluate your work or your partner's work in the Focus Practice Behaviors by completing the Practice Behaviors Assessment form below. What other Practice Behaviors did you use to complete these Exercises? Be sure to record them in your assessments.

1.	I have attained this competency/practice behavior (in the range of 80 to 100%)
2.	I have largely attained this competency/practice behavior (in the range of 60 to 80%)
3.	I have partially attained this competency/practice behavior (in the range of 40 to 60%)
4.	I have made a little progress in attaining this competency/practice behavior (in the range of 20 to 40%
5.	I have made almost no progress in attaining this competency/practice behavior (in the range of 0 to 20%)

EPAS 2008 Core Competencies & Core Practice Behaviors	Student Self Assessment						Evaluator Feedback
Student and Evaluator Assessment Scale and Comments	0	1	2	3	4	5	Agree/Disagree/Comments
2.1.1 Identity as a Professional Social Worker and Conduct Oneself Accordingly:							
a. Advocate for client access to the services of social work							
b. Practice personal reflection and self-correction to assure continual professional development							
c. Attend to professional roles and boundaries							

d. Demonstrate professional demeanor in behavior, appearance, and communication							
e. Engage in career-long learning							
f. Use supervision and consultation							
2.1.2 Apply Social Work Ethical Principles to Guide Professional Practice:							
a. Recognize and manage personal values in a way that allows professional values to guide practice							
b. Make ethical decisions by applying NASW Code of Ethics and, as applicable, IFSW/IASSW Ethics in Social Work, Statement of Principles							
c. Tolerate ambiguity in resolving ethical conflicts							
d. Apply strategies in resolving ethical conflicts							
2.1.3 Apply Critical Thinking to Inform and Communicate Professional Judgments:							
a. Distinguish, appraise, and integrate multiple sources of knowledge, including research-based knowledge and practice wisdom							
b. Analyze models of assessment, prevention, intervention, and evaluation							
c. Demonstrate effective oral and written communication in working with individuals, families, groups, organizations, communities, and colleagues							
2.1.4 Engage Diversity and Difference in Practice:							
a. Recognize the extent to which a culture's structures and values may oppress, marginalize, alienate, or create or enhance privilege and power							
b. Gain sufficient self-awareness to eliminate the influence of personal biases and values in working with diverse groups							
c. Recognize and communicate their understanding of the importance of difference in shaping life experiences							

d. View themselves as learners and engage those with whom they work as informants							
2.1.5 Advance Human Rights and Social and Economic Justice							
a. Understand forms and mechanisms of oppression and discrimination							
b. Advocate for human rights and social and economic justice							
c. Engage in practices that advance social and economic justice							
2.1.6 Engage in research-informed practice and practice-informed research							
a. Use practice experience to inform scientific inquiry							
b. Use research evidence to inform practice							
2.1.7 Apply knowledge of human behavior and the social environment:							
a. Utilize conceptual frameworks to guide the processes of assessment, intervention, and evaluation							
b. Critique and apply knowledge to understand person and environment							
2.1.8 Engage in policy practice to advance social and economic well-being and to deliver effective social work services:							
a. Analyze, formulate, and advocate for policies that advance social well-being							
b. Collaborate with colleagues and clients for effective policy action							
2.1.9 Respond to contexts that shape practice:							
a. Continuously discover, appraise, and attend to changing locales, populations, scientific and technological developments, and emerging societal trends to provide relevant services							
b. Provide leadership in promoting sustainable changes in service delivery and practice to improve the quality of social services							

2.1.10 Engage, assess, intervene, and evaluate with individuals, families, groups, organizations and communities:							
a. Substantively and affectively prepare for action with individuals, families, groups, organizations, and communities							
b. Use empathy and other interpersonal skills							
c. Develop a mutually agreed-on focus of work and desired outcomes							
d. Collect, organize, and interpret client data							
e. Assess client strengths and limitations							
f. Develop mutually agreed-on intervention goals and objectives							
g. Select appropriate intervention strategies.							
h. Initiate actions to achieve organizational goals							
i. Implement prevention interventions that enhance client capacities							
j. Help clients resolve problems							
k. Negotiate, mediate, and advocate for clients							
l. Facilitate transitions and endings							
m. Critically analyze, monitor, and evaluate interventions							

Direct Social Work Practice: Theory and Skills, 9th Edition

Aligned to
EPAS 2008 Competencies and Practice Behaviors

EPAS Competencies and Practice Behaviors:	Discussed in Chapter(s):	Assessed in Practice Behaviors Workbook Chapter:
2.1.1 Identify as a professional social worker and conduct oneself accordingly	1, 2, 3, 7	
a. Advocate for client access to the services of social work	2, 14, 18	14, 18
b. Practice personal reflection and self-correction to assure continual professional development	4, 5, 7, 12, 19	4, 19
c. Attend to professional roles and boundaries	2, 4, 5, 7, 10, 13, 18	10, 18
d. Demonstrate professional demeanor in behavior, appearance, and communication	4, 6, 7, 12, 14, 15, 18	14, 15, 18
e. Engage in career-long learning		
f. Use supervision and consultation	3, 4, 10, 12, 13, 18, 19	13, 18, 19

EPAS Competencies and Practice Behaviors: (continued…)	Discussed in Chapter(s):	Assessed in Practice Behaviors Workbook Chapter(s):
2.1.2 Apply social work ethical principles to guide professional practice	1	1
a. Recognize and manage personal values in a way that allows professional values to guide practice	1, 4, 10, 12, 14, 18	10, 12, 14, 18
b. Make ethical decisions by applying standards of the National Association of Social Workers *Code of Ethics* and, as applicable, of the International Federation of Social Workers/International Association of Schools of Social Work *Ethics in Social Work, Statement of Principles*	1, 4, 11, 12, 13, 18, 19	11, 12, 18, 19
c. Tolerate ambiguity in resolving ethical conflicts	4, 11	4, 11
d. Apply strategies in resolving ethical conflicts	4, 11, 13	4, 11, 13
2.1.3 Apply critical thinking to inform and communicate professional judgments	1, 3, 18	18
a. Distinguish, appraise, and integrate multiple sources of knowledge, including research-based knowledge and practice wisdom	8, 10, 19	8, 10, 19
b. Analyze models of assessment, prevention, intervention, and evaluation	1, 3, 8, 11, 13, 19	8, 11, 13, 19

- 240 -

EPAS Competencies and Practice Behaviors: (continued...)	Discussed in Chapter(s):	Assessed in Practice Behaviors Workbook Chapter(s):
c. Demonstrate effective oral and written communication in working with individuals, families, groups, organizations, communities, and colleagues	9	9
2.1.4 Engage diversity and difference in practice	1, 3	1
a. Recognize the extent to which a culture's structures and values may oppress, marginalize, alienate, or create or enhance privilege and power	10, 14, 15, 18	10, 14, 15, 18
b. Gain sufficient self-awareness to eliminate the influence of personal biases and values in working with diverse groups	3, 8, 10, 13, 14, 15, 18	8, 10, 13, 14, 15, 18
c. Recognize and communicate their understanding of the importance of difference in shaping life experiences	6, 7, 8, 9, 10, 11, 12, 13, 18	6, 8, 9, 10, 11, 12, 13, 18
d. View themselves as learners and engage those with whom they work as informants	6, 8, 13, 14, 18, 19	6, 8, 13, 14, 18, 19
2.1.5 Advance human rights and social and economic justice	2	1
a. Understand forms and mechanisms of oppression and discrimination	2, 10, 14, 18	10, 14, 18
b. Advocate for human rights and social and economic justice	1, 2, 14	14

EPAS Competencies and Practice Behaviors: (continued…)	Discussed in Chapter(s):	Assessed in Practice Behaviors Workbook Chapter(s):
c. Engage in practices that advance social and economic justice	1, 2, 14	14
2.1.6 Engage in research-informed practice and practice-informed research	1, 2	1
a. Use practice experience to inform scientific inquiry	2	
b. Use research evidence to inform practice	2, 11, 13, 14, 16, 18	11, 13, 14, 16, 18
2.1.7 Apply knowledge of human behavior and the social environment	1, 3	1
a. Utilize conceptual frameworks to guide the process of assessment, intervention, and evaluation	3, 8, 9, 10, 11, 13, 15, 16	3, 5, 8, 9, 10, 11, 13, 15, 16
b. Critique and apply knowledge to understand person and environment	3, 8, 9, 10, 12, 13, 15, 18	8, 9, 10, 13, 15, 18
2.1.8 Engage in policy practice to advance social and economic well-being and to deliver effective social work services	1, 2	
a. Analyze, formulate, and advocate for policies that advance social well-being	2, 14	14
b. Collaborate with colleagues and clients for effective policy action	2	

EPAS Competencies and Practice Behaviors: (continued…)	Discussed in Chapter(s):	Assessed in Practice Behaviors Workbook Chapter(s):
2.1.9 Respond to contexts that shape practice	1, 2	1, 2
a. Continuously discover, appraise, and attend to changing locales, populations, scientific and technological developments, and emerging societal trends to provide relevant services	2, 13, 14, 16	13, 14, 16
b. Provide leadership in promoting sustainable changes in service delivery and practice to improve the quality of social services	2, 14	14
2.1.10 Engage, assess, intervene, and evaluate with individuals, families, groups, organizations, and communities	1, 2, 3, 7, 16	3, 16
a. Substantively and affectively prepare for action with individuals, families, groups, organizations, and communities	1, 3, 4, 5, 6, 7, 8, 9, 10, 11, 12, 13, 14, 15, 16, 18	1, 2, 3, 4, 6, 8, 10, 11, 12, 13, 14, 15, 16, 18
b. Use empathy and other interpersonal skills	1, 3, 5, 6, 13, 14, 15, 17, 18, 19	3, 5, 13, 14, 15, 18, 19
c. Develop a mutually agreed-on focus of work and desired outcomes	1, 2, 12, 14, 15, 18	12, 14, 15, 18
d. Collect, organize, and interpret client data	1, 3, 6, 7, 8, 9, 10, 11, 12, 13, 14, 15	8, 9, 10, 11, 12, 13, 14, 15
e. Assess client strengths and limitations	1, 3, 5, 7, 8, 9, 10, 11, 12, 14, 15	8, 9, 10, 11, 12, 14, 15
f. Develop mutually agreed-on intervention goals and objectives	3, 13, 15	3, 13, 15

EPAS Competencies and Practice Behaviors: (continued)	Discussed in Chapter(s):	Assessed in Practice Behaviors Workbook Exercises:
g. Select appropriate intervention strategies	3, 6, 12, 13, 14, 16	12, 13, 14, 16
h. Initiate actions to achieve organizational goals	14	14
i. Implement prevention interventions that enhance client capacities	5, 12, 13, 16	12, 13, 16
j. Help clients resolve problems	3, 10, 11, 12, 13, 15, 16, 18	10, 11, 12, 13, 15, 16, 18
k. Negotiate, mediate, and advocate for clients	2, 3	2, 3
l. Facilitate transitions and endings	3, 16, 19	16, 19
m. Critically analyze, monitor, and evaluate interventions	3, 6, 12, 13, 18, 19	12, 13, 18, 19

CPSIA information can be obtained
at www.ICGtesting.com
Printed in the USA
FFOW03n1216150915
16926FF